Religion and Development in the Asia-Pacific

Community development is most effective and efficient when it is situated and led at the local level and considers the social behaviours, needs and worldviews of local communities. With more than eight out of ten people globally self-reporting religious belief, *Religion and Development in the Asia-Pacific: Sacred places as development spaces* argues that the role and impact of religions on community development needs to be better understood. It also calls for greater attention to be given to the role of sacred places as sites for development activities, and for a deeper appreciation of the way in which sacred stories and teachings inspire people to work for the benefit of others in particular locations.

The book considers theories of 'place' as a component of successful development interventions and expands this analysis to consider the specific role that sacred places – buildings and social networks – have in planning, implementing and promoting sustainable development. A series of case studies examine various sacred places as sites for development activities. These case studies include Christian churches and disaster relief in Vanuatu; Muslim shrines and welfare provision in Pakistan; a women's Buddhist monastery in Thailand advancing gender equity; a Jewish aid organisation providing language training to Muslim Women in Australia; and Hawaiian sacred sites located within a holistic retreat centre committed to ecological sustainability.

Religion and Development in the Asia-Pacific demonstrates the important role that sacred spaces can play in development interventions, covering diverse major world religions, interfaith and spiritual contexts, and as such will be of considerable interest for postgraduate students and researchers in development studies, religious studies, sociology of religion and geography.

Matthew Clarke is Head of the School of Humanities and Social Sciences, Deakin University, Australia.

Anna Halafoff is a Senior Lecturer in Sociology at Deakin University, Australia.

Routledge Research in Religion and Development

The *Routledge Research in Religion and Development* series focuses on the diverse ways in which religious values, teachings and practices interact with international development.

While religious traditions and faith-based movements have long served as forces for social innovation, it has only been within the last ten years that researchers have begun to seriously explore the religious dimensions of international development. However, recognising and analysing the role of religion in the development domain is vital for a nuanced understanding of this field. This interdisciplinary series examines the intersection between these two areas, focusing on a range of contexts and religious traditions.

Religion, Heritage and the Sustainable City
Hinduism and Urbanization in Jaipur
Yamini Narayanan

Religion and Urbanism
Reconceptualising sustainable cities for South Asia
Yamini Narayanan

Religions and Development in Asia
Sacred Places as Development Spaces
Matthew Clarke and Anna Halafoff

Religion and Development in the Asia-Pacific

Sacred places as development spaces

Matthew Clarke and Anna Halafoff

LONDON AND NEW YORK

First published 2017 by Routledge

2 Park Square, Milton Park, Abingdon, Oxfordshire OX14 4RN
711 Third Avenue, New York, NY 10017

Routledge is an imprint of the Taylor & Francis Group, an informa business

First issued in paperback 2018

British Library Cataloguing in Publication Data
A catalogue record for this book is available from the British Library

Library of Congress Cataloging in Publication Data
A catalog record for this title has been requested

ISBN: 978-1-138-79236-4 (hbk)
ISBN: 978-0-367-02708-7 (pbk)

Typeset in Sabon
by Taylor & Francis Books

For Clare and Noel (deceased) and Chris and Cosmo

Contents

Acknowledgement

The authors sincerely thank all of the participants who were interviewed for this project from the following organisations and communities: Presbyterian Women's Missionary Union, Minhaj-ul-Quran International, Songdhammakalyani Monastery, Kalani and StandUp.

We also thank our research assistant Jayne Garrod, and our families for their support and patience while we were undertaking fieldwork and writing up the research findings.

Preface

Concepts of space and place, religion and development are varied and contested depending on where and by whom they have been constructed. We begin with two individual reflections that situate us – the authors – and our ideas within the broader context of this study and explain our reasons for undertaking this inquiry.

More than 20 years ago, one of the authors of this book was working for a large international aid agency. Whilst based in Australia, the role performed required working with national offices of the same aid agency located in developing countries in identifying, planning and evaluating community development activities. The primary funding body for these activities was the Australian aid programme. At this time, a significant focus of the Australian government's aid programme in Thailand was on HIV and AIDS care and prevention. In the early 1990s, prevalence rates across the general Thai population were quite high, and in specific cohorts, such as commercial sex workers, they were alarming. Whilst the range of Australian government-funded projects was specific to each community, they were largely focused during this period on mass community education, the social marketing of condoms and home care of those with HIV and AIDS.

Whilst the author was based in Australia, he undertook regular travel to Thailand (in this case) to work with local staff and communities on these projects. As a relatively recent graduate with a freshly minted M.A. in Development Studies, he felt pretty confident on the theory of community development but at that time lacked experience of the lived reality of the communities with whom he was working. On reflection, there is no doubt that the author's level of naivety was considerable!

And so it was in this context of (presumed) strong theoretical knowledge alongside minimal experience in developing countries, that the author participated in an evaluation of a HIV and AIDS care and prevention programme being run with Muslim communities in southern Thailand. Working primarily in partnership with the nursing department of a local university, the programme aimed to increase the incidence of and improve the level of care of those in this Muslim community with HIV and AIDS. Without access to appropriate health care services and often with underlying poor health, it was common during the early 1990s in these circumstances for people to develop AIDS quite soon after contracting HIV. It was also very common for care of the ill to be undertaken by their own families or other members of their own community. Home care was therefore one of the core tenets of the care and prevention programmes funded by the Australian aid programme across Thailand.

The care that was provided by the families centred around improved nutrition and the cleaning of wounds associated with this condition. Given the nature of HIV transmission, there were high levels of risk for those providing this care. Thus, this particular funded activity, in conjunction with the nursing department, focused on providing training to Muslim women – who were the caregivers in this specific community – around safe dressing of wounds and disposal of potentially infected medical waste.

During the evaluation of this community development activity, it was apparent to the author that the training provided by the nursing department was of very high quality and was specifically tailored to the needs of this community and took into account the resources they had available to them on a daily basis. The nurses trained these caregivers across a wide range of topics, from dressing wounds, disposal of contaminated material, nutrition, exercise, mental well-being, and so forth. Indeed, the project clearly met all the goals that had been set at its inception and was clearly going to leave a community in which the ongoing care and prevention of HIV and AIDS was significantly improved from the experiences prior to the project commencing. In this regard, it was a very successful programme.

There was, though, one concern that troubled the author. According to the community development theory, of which he considered himself as having good knowledge, community development training initiatives should take place in environments that are non-threatening and familiar to the participants. Moreover, this training should be close to where the participants live and timed so as to not further burden them with additional work during busy periods of either the day (i.e. preparation of meals or caring of family members) or year (i.e. during periods of harvest). The prevailing community development theory taught at that time held that taking people away from their own environments could intimidate them, reduce their ability to learn new information, minimise participation, and thus render the training ineffective. Thus, it was problematic for the author that in the face of this theory the programme activities required the Muslim women to be bussed from their own communities to the university campus so that the nurses could undertake the training at the university itself. Given the existing constraints placed on their mobility because of religious traditions and their own limited education opportunities, placing them in a university setting appeared completely incongruent with what the author had been so recently taught at his own university. Surely, he presumed, these women would be overwhelmed by this unfamiliar environment, which would hinder their ability to learn the material being taught. It also, he further concluded, preferenced the needs and time of the nurse-trainers over the commitments of the women themselves who had to absent themselves from their own community for these training sessions. This was, the author felt, a major failing of the project and would need to be addressed and corrected in future funded programmes of this nature.

Localised training was appropriate and proper according to contemporary community development theory. And so, given the flagrant disregard for appropriate places and spaces for training in this programme, the author proceeded to raise his concerns with the programme staff, the nurse-trainers and the Muslim women themselves. What was soon learned was shocking to him. Prior to the training, these women were, because of their cultural practices, largely confined to their own homes, unable to leave without male chaperones. Thus, they were excluded from many social activities, including simple daily tasks such as shopping and taking children to school. However, having gone through the HIV and AIDS care and prevention training at the university, attitudes towards these women within their own families and communities shifted markedly. One woman described how her husband now allowed her to undertake the family shopping in the local markets on her own as she now had a 'university-education' and had a better education than himself! Indeed, as a result of travelling outside of their own communities to the university, these women were afforded much greater freedom and given greater respect for having undertaken this training in such a specialised space and unfamiliar place. All participants reported the location at the university as playing a significant role in their increased knowledge and skills as well as the unexpected enhanced freedom of movement and respect within their own communities. It was quite evident that had the training occurred at a local place and a familiar space, these increased freedoms would not have been achieved. These women self-reported that these freedoms were of equal value to the increased knowledge gained around care and prevention of HIV and AIDS.

Whilst simply anecdotal, this experience did impress upon the author the possibility that community development theory around place and space may need to be challenged and reconsidered. Over the next two decades though, little work has taken place within the development studies literature on place and space. In practice, community development activities are largely undertaken in localised and familiar settings. Examination of the power of place and space though remains under-researched. The experiences over two decades ago in Hat Yai, Thailand remain core as to the geneses of this book.

* * *

When the second author first enrolled in a Master of Letters in Peace Studies in 2000, focusing on religion, peace and conflict, the standard responses from people were disparaging comments such as 'what are you doing that for?', 'that is so esoteric', 'you will never get a job'. Yet after the tragic events of September 11, 2001, there weren't many people in Australia with such qualifications and their expertise was in high demand.

The M.Litt. that this author undertook was multidisciplinary and featured courses in geography, development studies, economics, international relations, conflict resolution and peace studies. Much of the content was centred on so-called developing nations and understanding the underlying causes of local and global conflicts. These included colonisation, capitalism, and resulting social and environmental exploitation and degradation.

The content on development in the M.Litt. both fascinated and troubled the author.

The importance of religion in development and international affairs was beginning to be acknowledged by scholars and international agencies in the 1990s. Douglas Johnston and Cynthia Sampson's edited collection *Religion, The Missing Dimension of Statecraft* was published by Oxford University Press in 1994, and James D. Wolfensohn, then president of the World Bank co-founded The World Faiths Development Dialogue with Lord George Carey, the then Archbishop of Canterbury in 1998. The global multifaith movement was also gathering momentum at the end of the twentieth century responding to human and environmental crisis events.

What the author struggled with was that the development field and the 2000 Millennium Development Goals were largely focused on addressing issues of poverty, health and education in 'non-Western' societies. However she was growing painfully aware through the content of the M.Litt. that many of the troubles facing these societies and the world at large were produced by Western nations, which also had serious problems with structural violence, including gender, sexuality and cultural inequalities, and with sustainable development. She therefore chose to focus more on her own backyard, so to speak, at this time and embarked upon further studies in the sociology of religion.

Since the mid-2000s the author's research has been primarily concerned with religious diversity and governance. She has documented and analysed the rise of the multifaith movement and of multi-actor peacebuilding networks in Western nations in response to global risks of terrorism and climate change at the turn of the twenty-first century. More recently she has focused on researching state government approaches to education about diverse religions and non-religious worldviews in Australia and other nations and regions such as the UK, the EU and Canada.

While this author has been fortunate to have visited many sacred sites while conducting research on and with diverse faith communities, or while pursuing her own spiritual and religious interests, she hasn't investigated the construction of or use of places or of spaces in her previous studies. The author's own understanding of sacred places and development spaces is very much influenced by her travels and experiences, and most recently by her reading of Dzogchen Buddhist texts.

When the author thinks of places which are sacred to her they are all natural spaces: Fowlers Beach on the Mornington Peninsula and the Dandenong Ranges on the outskirts of Melbourne where she spent a good deal of her childhood playing in rockpools and listening out for lyrebirds; Clarkes Beach in Byron Bay and Myall Beach in Cape Tribulation where she lived as a young adult and really did her growing up; Chenrezig Institute in Eudlo, the Tibetan Buddhist

Centre in a sub-tropical rainforest setting that became her spiritual home in her thirties and the Bodhi tree at Bodhgaya, in India, the place where Buddha reached enlightenment that she went on a pilgrimage to a few years ago.

These places are imbued with cultural and personal significance; they are full of stories, her stories and those of others who share an affinity with them. Being in nature offers the author the possibility of slowing down, of reflection, of marveling in the wonder of natural beauty and at times its brutality. She feels deeply connected to these places and the communities who inhabit them, both non-human and human. She receives daily updates from friends and organisations on social media who are situated near these sacred sites. These images and notifications keep her links with them alive, even when she's not there. She strongly believes that we need to work together on protecting wilderness areas and sacred places, which are currently being threatened by climate change and terror. We must also confront underlying social problems of greed, inequity and prejudice that fuel these crises and we still need to better understand religion's role in creating, perpetuating and countering them.

On a recent trip to Washington, to attend the President's Interfaith and Community Service Campus Challenge, she was informed about the 2015 Sustainable Development Goals. While maintaining a similar focus to their previous iteration on ending poverty, improving gender equality and sustainability, the SDGs recognise that local and global social and environmental risks are present in and threaten all societies and that we must create partnerships across diverse sectors to confront them and to create more sustainable and harmonious communities. Hearing about the SDGs reignited the author's interest in development studies and religion.

* * *

This book, on sacred places as development spaces, also takes a wide view of development in economically poorer and richer societies. Our case studies examine sacred places in Vanuatu, Pakistan, Thailand, Australia and Hawai'i. We investigate projects in these locations centred on gender equity, disaster management, education, environmental and spiritual development, and eradicating poverty and hunger. The sacred sites and communities we explore include Christian, Muslim, Buddhist, Jewish and spiritual communities. Some of our case studies also include discussions of these organisation's websites.

Place and space are important, but within development studies they have not been afforded the consideration they require. It is hoped that this book may address the issues that challenged both authors and help better inform the understanding of space and place within community development theory and practice.

Introduction

At the turn of this century, global leaders publically committed to significantly improving the wellbeing of the world's poorest and most vulnerable. A series of development targets – known as the Millennium Development Goals (MDGs) – were specified including eradicating extreme poverty and hunger, providing universal primary education, increasing gender equality, improving maternal and child health, and combating illnesses such as HIV and AIDS. The value of the MDGs was in large part that for the first time, timelines were set by nearly 200 world leaders to achieve these goals and their attainment was explicitly made the responsibility of both rich and poor countries (United Nations n.d.).

Now, more than 15 years later and with the time period during which these goals were to be achieved having passed, it is possible to see great improvements in wellbeing for hundreds of millions of the world's poor. Across the globe, the gap between the number of people not living in absolute poverty and those that are is greater than ever in human history (Roser 2015). Since 2000, around one billion people were lifted out of absolute poverty primarily through a growth in income. Greater numbers of children survived past their fifth birthday and increasing numbers were able to access primary education (World Bank 2015). However, despite these wonderful achievements, around 10 per cent of the global population – 700 million people – remain in absolute poverty. And whilst extreme hunger was reduced by over 40 per cent since 1990, there remain 800 million people across the globe who are undernourished (FAO 2014). Those experiencing this extreme poverty and hunger have become increasingly concentrated in Sub-Saharan Africa and South Asia. In addition, there are still hundreds of millions of people vulnerable to falling back into absolute poverty if their economic circumstances decline slightly. Environmental or political shocks could thus reverse many of the gains of the past 15 years of focused international efforts.

At the global level, the international community has continued its commitment to addressing this ongoing poverty through what have been recently announced as the Sustainable Development Goals (SDGs). The SDGs focus on ending poverty and hunger, promoting health and wellbeing, quality education, gender equality, sustainable water management, economic growth, responsible consumption and production, combating climate change and promoting peaceful and inclusive societies (United Nations 2015).

Precisely how individuals and communities understand and respond to these circumstances of poverty and hunger and indeed to evolving economic, social, political and environment systems at the local level is dependent on their wider view of the world and on their own place within it. The fact therefore that around 85 per cent of the world's population professes religious belief (Pew Research Centre 2012) becomes increasingly relevant in the forming of worldviews and thus the reaction to global as well as private experiences of poverty and hunger. According to more than 2,500 population surveys and censuses, it is estimated that nearly one-third of the global population (2.2 billion people) self-profess as Christian, just under a quarter of the world's population (1.6 billion people) are Muslim, 15 per cent (one billion people) are Hindus and 500 million (7 per cent) of the global population identify as Buddhist. A similar number of people practice traditional or folk religions. Such numbers suggest that religious belief is a central human characteristic that can be found in all societies, in all parts of the world and across recorded human existence. In this sense, religious belief is not only profound, it is also pervasive, persistent and persuasive. Religion is therefore not exotic, but is very much a part of the social context that should be routinely considered when undertaking development interventions.

With religious belief being so common, particularly within developing countries, considering the potential impact such beliefs have on the worldviews of individuals and societies – specifically with regards to the experience of poverty and efforts to alleviate such poverty and hunger – should also be common practice. However, until relatively recently it has been poorly understood and undervalued largely due to processes of secularisation which sidelined religions to the more private sphere. A series of global crisis events involving religion have recently challenged this position and there is no doubt that the public presence of religion increased at the turn of the twenty-first century, largely as a result of processes of globalisation and mediatisation of these risks. This has led to a need to take religion more seriously and a corresponding increase of research on religions across many disciplines including development studies, media studies, sociology, politics and geography.

The global spread of people, goods and ideas across spaces has led not only to a rise in religiously diverse societies, but also to a growing visibility of religion and awareness of this diversity. The demographics of many societies are shifting to include more religious minorities, new religions and also more people declaring to have no religious affiliation. A wide assortment of temples, mosques, gurdwaras and churches can be found in numerous major cities and regional centres throughout the world (Bouma 2006; Hedges and Halafoff 2015). Many of these places regularly celebrate their religious diversity with festivals and promote educational programmes to instill respect for diverse cultures and religions and to aid interreligious understanding. These activities are widely advertised and reported in local papers. State actors, in partnership with community leaders, have developed multicultural and multifaith policies and strategies for managing and governing religious diversity and maintaining socially cohesive societies (Bouma 1995, 1997; Bader 2007), which are published and disseminated on their websites. At the same time, diverse religious communities are increasing their presence in the public sphere and are involved in governance of their own communities and of society at large (Habermas 2006; Halafoff 2013). While many people welcome these developments, others have strongly resisted them.

Throughout the world, at the same time as we have witnessed a growing cosmopolitan consciousness, embracing diversity while cognisant of the need to respect the rights of others, we have also witnessed a hardening of attitudes against migrants and refugees, rising xenophobia and the wish to protect 'our way of life' from the dangerous Other. These processes are deeply intertwined as the more movement there is across spaces, and the more open they become, the more some people's ontological security is threatened (Kaldor 1999; Beckford 2003; Beck 2006; Halafoff 2013). This is in a sense nothing new; racism, religious vilification and fear of others have long been present in society, yet processes of globalisation and mediatisation have accelerated change and fears exponentially. We are now so much more aware of what is happening both in our own communities and in other societies. Yet not everyone is willing to embrace the reality of the interconnectedness and interdependent nature of the lifeworld, and challenges to the very notion that there is an Other. Instead, tribal boundaries are being constructed with a new vehemence and religious identity is one of the strongest markers of in-groups and out-groups (Habermas 1998; Kaldor 2003; Bouma 2006; Halafoff 2013).

In addition, these fears have been compounded by very real risks confronting local and global societies. Global inequalities and gaps between rich and poor are persistent problems. Once again, the internet and spread of global and social media makes us ever aware of these inequities and the intersections of many forms of oppression and discrimination within societies based on gender, class, race and religion. Poverty, gender-based and sexuality-based violence, racial and religious vilification are issues that confront all societies, categorised as developed or developing. Modernity and capitalism have broken their promises to deliver a fairer and more equal world and have been increasingly questioned as a result (Beckford 2003; Willaime 2006; Halafoff 2013).

While these risks no doubt further fuel fears and prejudices, they have also created new spaces to challenge them. Indeed, the rising awareness of risks and global crises is cited as a significant factor of the increase in interest in religions, both peaceful and conservative at the end of the twentieth century. As people, and young people in particular, became disillusioned with capitalism they sought alternative frameworks for understanding how to create more equal and harmonious societies. Religions have long provided such maps, providing answers to life's big questions and instructions on how to improve one's self and to create a better world. Religions also focus on helping those in need and less fortunate (McGuire 1997; Campbell 2006). The late 2000s saw a rise in many religious social movements, and movements that weren't necessarily religious but were motivated at least in part by religious and/or spiritual ideology, such as the environmental movement, confronting pressing issues (Habermas 1981; Bainbridge 1997). Some were peaceful, others militant. Some were socially progressive and others were conservative, and even fundamentalist. Yet all shared a similar goal of replacing capitalist modernity with other ideologies that they thought and felt would create better societies (Marty and Appleby 1992; Casanova 1994, 2001; Halafoff 2013).

The rise of Islamist social movements and the tragic events of September 11, 2001 and the 2002 and 2005 Bali, 2004 Madrid, 2005 London and 2009 Mumbai terrorist attacks propelled religion to the forefront of the public mind (Halafoff 2013; Kong 2010). The more recent formation of Islamic State and their attacks in France, Tunisia, Australia and the US have also generated a considerable amount of media, government and UN attention regarding how best to understand the role of religion within this movement and to counter violent extremism.

As religions began to play a more public role in society and in conflicts at the turn of the twenty-first century, state actors, non-government and inter-governmental agencies realised they needed to start taking religion more seriously. Processes of secularisation and secularisation theory had led to a devaluing of the importance of religion in public life by scholars, state actors and global organisations such as the UN in the earlier part of the twentieth century (Beckford 1990; Casanova 1994; Taylor 2009). During the 1980s and particularly in the 1990s a significant shift occurred in which peacebuilding partnerships were formed between state and global organisations and religious communities in order to confront common crises in fields of diplomacy, international relations and development. These peacebuilding partnerships and the need to understand religion and to partner with religious leaders in countering threats of violent extremism became even more critical following the September 11, 2001 and the 2005 London bombings. Notable examples include the World Bank's World Faiths Development Dialogue, the UN's Tripartite Forum on Interfaith Cooperation for Peace, and the World Economic Forum's Council of 100 and Global Agenda Council on the Role of Faith (Appleby 2000, 2003; Marshall and Keough 2004; Halafoff 2013).

Given continued risks of poverty, terrorism and climate change, the problems and issues we now face in the mid-2010s remain similar to the ones faced in the 1990s and 2000s. Yet the hope and faith that many people had in religion as a positive force of social change is in many places diminishing. This is occurring at least in part due to an outcry against conservative and fundamentalist forms of religion's influence in the public sphere, with growing calls for a strengthening of secular governance globally. Numbers of religious 'nones', those declaring no religious affiliation, are rising as is the public critique of religion and popularity of movements such as New Atheism (Kettell 2013). Religions' association with violence, both direct and structural, including acts of terror and inquiries into sexual abuse of children, have led to a public interrogation of religious teachings and practices which contravene human rights that many will agree has been highly necessary. Religious organisations and leaders have become much more accountable to state officials and to the public through media scrutiny. Religion's role in creating and perpetuating acts of violence has also been the subject of a considerable amount of scholarship and policy analysis. These are no doubt welcome developments, yet the positive role of religion in peacebuilding and development remains eclipsed by negative reporting by the media and emphasis in academic inquiry on religion and conflict. This public attack on religion, and Islam in particular has also led to widespread Islamophobia and migrantophobia across Western societies, as people ignorantly equate all Muslims and migrants with extremist movements. This has led to calls for much needed educational programmes to build a greater understanding of diverse religions and worldviews and more socially inclusive societies, mitigating clashes not only between religious actors but between religious and non-religious individuals and groups (Halafoff 2013; Jackson 2014).

The global risk of climate change has also gathered momentum in the mid-2010s. Extreme weather events as part of climate change have had devastating effects on societies. Environmental risks also intersect with social risks and can lead to and certainly exacerbate conflicts. Religion's role in creating, exacerbating and ameliorating environmental crises has also attracted significant scholarly attention (Kearns and Keller 2007; Halafoff 2013; FORE n.d.). Partnerships have also been forming between religious and non-religious actors, and states, NGOs and the UN to work for sustainable development (Kearns and Keller 2007; Halafoff 2013).

What must also be noted is that the increased public prominence of religion, and the preoccupation with religion and human and environmental security has led scholars in more recent years to develop theories that were focused less on official and sensational aspects of religion, and their policy implications, but more on everyday, lived and embodied experiences of religion and spirituality.

Meredith McGuire's (2008) research on lived religion found people's expressions and experiences of religion to be diverse, complex, malleable and contradictory. McGuire (2008, p. 13) argued, drawing upon Nancy Ammerman's (1996, 2003) and Robert Orsi's (2005) work, that 'embodied practices' link the material and spiritual aspects of people's lives and that individual religion, through shared practices and meanings, is 'fundamentally social'. Ammerman's (2007, 2013a) studies of religion in everyday life discovered the sacred to be present in the home, in illness and health care, in the arts, and in volunteering. People prayed, wore religious symbols, got tattoos, had religious images in their houses, spoke with the dead, went on pilgrimages, and took part in religious gatherings and healing rituals where they thought of the sacred and the secular, the ordinary and the extraordinary as intertwined and intermingled.

In contemporary societies, religion in its everyday, lived, embodied forms, and in its more public manifestations and discourses be they violent or peaceful, is ever present. In our digital age religions are also increasingly visible online, with religious online communities supplementing, rather than substituting real-world religious participation (Campbell 2005). Scholars of religion and the internet are examining issues of religious identity, authority, community, activism, and ritual in online spaces (Campbell 2012), with many of them focusing on everyday lived religious and spiritual experiences on websites, games and social media platforms as well as issues of radicalisation and countering violent extremism.

Scholarship on the internet and religion, and in this case religion and virtual spaces, is an expanding field and the importance of this inquiry has been recognised by international agencies such as the World Economic Forum's Global Agenda Council on the Role of Faith 2014–2015 as a priority area.

Religion's continued presence in public and more private spaces, and the increasingly blurred boundary between them has also led scholars to rethink notions of religion, spirituality and the sacred. While religion is typically viewed as organised, communal and traditional and in decline, spirituality is often seen to be more individual, innovative and on the rise, yet it is not that simple (Ammerman 2013b). Many people equate spirituality with religious participation, and religion and spirituality both place importance on meaning, relationships and community, as well as rituals and embodied practices (Ammerman 2013b; Woodhead 2011). The sacred is increasingly being used as a term to encompass not only religious and spiritual but also non-religious spaces, people, objects and experiences that we hold dear and/or that are transformative (Anttonen 2003 cited in Knott 2005), and/or in which there is a sensing of a presence greater than oneself (Hervieu-Léger 2000 cited in Knott 2005).

It is within this broader context of religion in public and more private places that our inquiry is situated. Our understanding of sacred places as development spaces is informed by the sociological scholarship on religion in the public sphere, religion and globalisation, religion and governance, religion, peace and conflict, religion and risk and everyday lived religion and the sacred presented above. A more detailed examination of theories of religion and development, and religion and geography focused on substantial and situational definitions of the sacred and the politics and poetics of space and place (Chidester and Linenthal 1995; Kong 2001, 2010) is included in the following chapter and then applied to our case studies across the Asia Pacific region.

Our case studies include: a Christian organisation's disaster management in Port Vila, Vanuatu; a Sufi Muslim welfare foundation's work around shrines in Lahore, Pakistan; a women's Buddhist monastery on the outskirts of Bangkok, Thailand, devoted to gender equity; a Jewish aid organisation embowering Muslim refugee women working out of a Christian church in the multifaith city of Dandenong, Australia; and a retreat centre in Puna, Hawai'i, committed to ecologically sustainable and holistic personal development. We have researched each site, community and/or organisation employing a mixed methods approach including participant observation and/or semi-structured interviews and website analysis, with ethics approval from Deakin University and with consent from each participant involved. The methods and numbers of participants for each study vary depending on the context, yet each resulting chapter explores the same theme of how sacred places are used as development spaces.

We have taken an inclusive approach regarding the sacred, the spiritual and the religious in our study, which, we have learned through our exploration of literature and online and off-line, places can be observed in more formal and obvious sites such as temples, churches, and shrines *and* in everyday, lived moments and settings. We have discovered that boundaries between binaries of sacred and profane, developed and developing, virtual and real are becoming increasingly blurry and porous.

We have also found that religious and/or spiritual frameworks for understanding the human condition and the world we live in inform the construction of sacred places in natural and urban settings and the development activities that take place within and around them. There is also no doubt that these frameworks, development places and activities are deeply relational and this will be discussed in more detail in the following chapters.

References

Ammerman, N. 1996, 'Organized religion in a voluntaristic society', *Sociology of Religion*, vol. 58, no. 3, pp. 203–215.

Ammerman, N. 2003, 'Religious identities and institutions', in M. Dillon (ed.), *Handbook of the sociology of religion*, Cambridge University Press, Cambridge, pp. 207–224.

Ammerman, N. 2007, *Everyday religion: Observing modern religious lives*, Oxford University Press, Oxford.

Ammerman, N. 2013a, *Sacred stories, spiritual tribes: Finding religion in everyday life*, Oxford University Press, New York.

Ammerman, N. 2013b, 'Spiritual but not religious? Beyond binary choices in the study of religion', *Journal for the Scientific Study of Religion*, vol. 52, no. 2, pp. 258–278.

Anttonen, V. 2003, 'Sacred sites as markers of difference – Exploring cognitive foundations of territoriality', in L. Tarkka (ed.), *Dynamics of tradition: Perspectives on oral poetry and folk belief*, The Finnish Literature Society, Helsinki, pp. 291–305.

Appleby, S.R. 2000, *The ambivalence of the sacred: Religion, violence, and reconciliation*, Rowman and Littlefield, Lanham.

Appleby, S.R. 2003, 'Retrieving the missing dimension of statecraft: Religious faith in the service of peacebuilding', in D. Johnston (ed.), *Faith-based diplomacy: Trumping realpolitik*, Oxford University Press, Oxford, pp. 231–258.

Bader, V. 2007, *Secularism or democracy? Associational governance of religious diversity*, Amsterdam University Press, Amsterdam.

Bainbridge, W.S. 1997, *The sociology of religious movements*, Routledge, New York.

Beck, U. 2006, *The cosmopolitan vision*, Polity Press, Cambridge.

Beckford, J.A. 1990, 'The sociology of religion and social problems', *Sociological Analysis*, vol. 51, no. 1, pp. 1–14.

Beckford, J.A. 2003, *Social theory and religion*, Cambridge University Press, Cambridge.

Bouma, G.D. 1995, 'The emergence of religious plurality in Australia: A multicultural society', *Sociology of Religion*, vol. 56, no. 4, pp. 285–302.

Bouma, G.D. (ed.) 1997, *Many religions, all Australian: Religious settlement, identity and cultural diversity*, The Christian Research Association, Melbourne.

Bouma, G.D. 2006, *Australian soul: Religion and spirituality in the 21st century*, Cambridge University Press, Cambridge.

Campbell, H. 2005, *Exploring religious community online: We are one in the network*, Peter Lang, New York.

Campbell, H. (ed.) 2012, *Digital religion: Understanding religious practice in new media worlds*, Routledge, London and New York.

Campbell, R.A. 2006, 'Theodicy, distribution of risk, and reflexive modernisation: Explaining the cultural significance of new religious movements', in J.A. Beckford &

J. Walliss (eds.), *Theorising religion: Classical and contemporary debates*, Ashgate, Aldershot, pp. 90–104.

Casanova, J. 1994, *Public religions in the modern world*, University of Chicago Press, Chicago.

Casanova, J. 2001, 'Religion, the new millennium, and globalization', *Sociology of Religion*, vol. 62, no. 4, pp. 415–441.

Chidester, D. & Linenthal, E.T. 1995, 'Introduction', in D. Chidester & E.T. Linenthal (eds.), *American sacred space*, Indiana University Press, Bloomington, pp. 1–42.

Food and Agricultural Organization (FAO) 2014, *The state of food insecurity in the world 2014: Strengthening the enabling Environment for food security and nutrition*, viewed 20 November 2015, http://www.fao.org/publications/sofi/2014/en.

Forum on Religion and Ecology (FORE) n.d., *Forum on religion and ecology at Yale University*, viewed 20 December 2015, http://fore.yale.edu.

Habermas, J. 1981, 'New social movements', *Telos*, vol. 49, pp. 33–37.

Habermas, J. 1998, 'Learning by disaster? A diagnostic look back on the short 20th century,' *Constellations*, vol. 5, no. 3, pp. 307–320.

Habermas, J. 2006, 'Religion in the public sphere', *European Journal of Philosophy*, vol. 14, no. 1, pp. 1–25.

Halafoff, A. 2013, *The multifaith movement: Global risks and cosmopolitan solutions*. Springer, Dordrecht.

Hedges, P. & Halafoff, A. 2015, 'Globalisation and multifaith societies', *Studies in Interreligious Dialogue*, vol. 25, no. 2, pp. 135–161.

Hervieu-Léger, D. 2000, *Religion as a chain of memory*, Polity, Cambridge.

Jackson, R. 2014, *'Signposts': Policy and practice for teaching about religions and non-religious worldviews in intercultural education*, Council of Europe, Strasbourg.

Kaldor, M. 1999, *New & old wars: Organized violence in a global era*, Polity, Cambridge.

Kaldor, M. 2003, *Global civil society: An answer to war*, Polity, Cambridge.

Kearns, L. & Keller, C. (eds.) 2007, *Ecospirit: Religions and philosophies for the earth*, Fordham University Press, New York.

Kettell, S. 2013, 'Faithless: The politics of New Atheism', *Secularism and Nonreligion*, vol. 2, pp. 61–72.

Knott, K. 2005, *The location of religion: A spatial analysis*, Equinox, London.

Kong, L. 2001, 'Mapping "new" geographies of religion: Politics and poetics in modernity', *Progress in Human Geography*, vol. 25, no. 2, pp. 211–233.

Kong, L. 2010, 'Global shifts, theoretical shifts: Changing geographies of religion', *Progress in Human Geography*, vol. 34, no. 6, pp. 755–776.

Marshall, K. & Keough, L. 2004, *Mind, heart, and soul in the fight against poverty*, The World Bank, Washington.

Marty, M.E. & Appleby, R.S. 1992, *The glory and the power: The fundamentalist challenge to the modern world*, Beacon Press, Boston.

McGuire, M. 1997, *Religion: The social context*, Belmont, Wadsworth.

McGuire, M. 2008, *Lived religion, faith and practice in everyday life*, Oxford University Press, Oxford.

Orsi, R.A. 2005, *Between heaven and earth: The religious world's people make and the scholars who study hem*, Princeton University Press, Princeton.

Pew Research Centre 2012, *Global religious landscape*, viewed 20 November 2015, http://www.pewforum.org/files/2014/01/global-religion-full.pdf.

Roser, M. (2015) 'World Poverty', *OurWorldInData.org*, viewed 20 November 2015, http://ourworldindata.org/data/growth-and-distribution-of-prosperity/world-poverty.

Taylor, C. 2009, 'Foreword: What is secularism?' in GB Levey & T Modood (eds.), *Secularism, religion and multicultural citizenship*, Cambridge University Press, Cambridge, pp. xi–xxii.

United Nations n. d., *Millenium development goals*, viewed 20 December 2015, http://www.un.org/millenniumgoals.

United Nations 2015, *Sustainable development goals*, viewed 20 December 2015, http://www.un.org/sustainabledevelopment/sustainable-development-goals.

Willaime, J.P. 2006, 'Religion in ultramodernity', in J.A. Beckford & J. Walliss (eds.), *Theorising religion: Classical and contemporary debates*, Ashgate, Aldershot, pp. 77–89.

World Bank 2015, *Global monitoring report 2015/2016: Development goals in an era of demographic change*, viewed 20 November 2015, http://pubdocs.worldbank.org/pubdocs/publicdoc/2015/10/503001444058224597/Global-Monitoring-Report-2015.pdf.

Woodhead, L. 2011, 'Five concepts of religion', *International Review of Sociology: Revue Internationale de Sociologie*, vol. 21, no. 1, pp. 121–143.

1 Religion, development and geography

Religion and development

Religious belief and practice is defined by Eliezer Segal (2009, p. 4) as 'the worship of a personal supernatural deity, a revealed scripture, a divinely ordained code of laws, and an assortment of institutions and communal structures in which the religion is observed'. As described briefly in our introduction, teachings and tenets associated with these religious beliefs therefore affect how individuals and societies conceive of the world. Certainly whilst core to this religious belief and practice is achieving a rightful relationship with a supernatural deity or deities, in most religions this relationship also requires achieving correct relationships within the temporal sphere. This temporal dimension of religious belief and practice necessarily results in religion being quite central to (at the least the aspirations of) how religious persons conduct their lives on a daily basis. The circumstances in which individuals find themselves – including their economic, social, political and environmental conditions – may well be reasonably understood in light of their own religious beliefs. As such, how they (or indeed, wider societies) respond to poverty and hunger (either their own or that experienced by others) may be shaped by the tenets, precepts, and social teaching of their religion. In this way, religious belief is not just a private concern in terms of an individual seeking to establish a rightful relationship with a deity or deities – important as that is – but does have wider impact across societies on social change. This impact is not simply corralled though to understanding the world and our place in it, but extends to addressing the inequities of the world.

Religious practices do result in concrete actions by those professing religious beliefs to positively impact upon the wellbeing of others. Matthew Clarke (2011) notes that the world's major religious traditions of Christianity, Islam, Hinduism, Buddhism and Judaism all make clear the responsibilities of adherents to respond to poverty, hunger and injustice in very real and material ways.[1] In each of these major religions, concepts of charity, welfare, environmental stewardship, social justice so forth are core tenets and precepts. Given the on-going material needs of the world's most vulnerable, religious belief and practice may be a powerful force in local and international efforts to alleviate such poverty and hunger. The process that drives such alleviation that in modern times is called 'development' shares many goals of equity and justice found in traditional and contemporary religious teachings across the globe.

Development is the process of achieving 'good change' (McGillivray 2012) or what Amartya Sen (1999) refers to as 'freedoms'. This good change or enhancement of freedom allows people to have greater choice in their lives: 'The most critical ones are to lead a long and healthy life, to be educated, and to enjoy a decent standard of living. If these essential choices are not available, many other opportunities remain inaccessible' (UNDP 1990, p. 10). While direct observation of these choices is difficult, various proxy indicators are widely used to encapsulate people's expression of these choices. Such proxy indicators include income, health indices, literacy rates or composite indicators of such indicators – including, for example, the Human Development Index. The process of development advances human dignity, social equity and self-determination. Where development is lacking, it is possible to observe social exclusion, ill-health, economic insecurity, and powerlessness.

According to Jim Ife (2013), the best community development outcomes are achieved when communities themselves own the process of both identifying their needs and the interventions designed to address these needs. This requires participatory representation, transparency and accountability mechanisms to underpin any efforts to improve the choices and freedoms of those whose lives are seeking to be affected. Community participation and ownership within development interventions have become widely accepted as the minimum requirement for successful and sustained development outcomes (see Chambers 2005). International financial institutions, multilateral agencies, national governments and NGOs have, by and large, incorporated the terms 'participation' and 'ownership' into their development jargon and practice (see Chambers 1983; Stiglitz 1999; Craig and Porter 1997; Sihlongonyane 2003). It is unlikely that any impact of the particular intervention will persist without active community involvement (as compared to passive acceptance) in all stages of development, including needs analysis, project identification and design, implementation, monitoring and evaluation (see Clarke et al. 2014). This is because the inclusion of those directly affected groups in the planning stages will more likely ensure that the right development needs and their causes are identified, and the responses planned will better take into account local resources and strengths of the local communities that will ensure that there is less reliance on external inputs. Finally, community participation will also aid in the on-going management of the project, as the decision-making processes will have been developed in the initial stages to include the relevant local beneficiaries and key stakeholders, which will continue once the external funding has ceased. Such improvements in choices and freedoms are also best achieved when explicit consideration is given to gender, the environment, and diversity within communities (including ethnic and religious minorities and those with disability). When development requires external interventions – such as those funded and facilitated by government authorities, NGOs or civil-based organisations (CBOs) – a focus on and appreciation of existing endogenous strengths is crucial to understanding existing deficits. To be successful in achieving long-term benefit, community development interventions seeking to enhance the wellbeing of communities must, finally, be firmly embedded in the cultural and religious experiences of those communities and be fully cognisant of how these communities understand the world and their own circumstances. However the relationship between religion and development has been somewhat fraught since the inception of the so-called development sector.

A brief history of 'development'

Seeking to improve one's own life and the circumstances of the wider community has driven human society for millennia. Indeed, this innate drive for greater social, physical and economic security has underpinned all advances in human history. Yet, it has only been since partway through the last century that a systematic process named as 'development' has been identified as an important aspect of relations between states and expressed responsibility of state leaders. Following the successful reconstruction of war-devastated Europe under the largely US-funded Marshall Plan, the international community focused its attention on the newly emerging states resulting from the process of de-colonisation occurring across Asia, Africa and Latin America (Kingsbury et al. 2011). President Harry S. Truman's 1949 Inauguration address is largely recognised as the starting point of the international community's commitment to improving the lives of the world's poor beyond the boundaries of individual countries. Truman (1949, p. 1) stated:

> ... we must embark on a bold new program for making the benefits of our scientific advances and industrial progress available for the improvement and growth of underdeveloped areas... More than half the people of the world are living in conditions approaching misery. Their food is inadequate. They are victims of disease. Their economic life is primitive and stagnant. Their poverty is a handicap and a threat both to them and to more prosperous areas... Our aim should be to help the free peoples of the world, through their own efforts, to produce more food, more clothing, more materials for housing, and more mechanical power to lighten their burdens.

Pure altruism was of course not a sole driver of this new-found determination to improve the material lives of the poor. Almost immediately, 'development' was mired in Cold War politics with both the West and East supporting political and social development throughout the globe as strategic aspects of their own international interests. That notwithstanding, it is clear that aid flows and other financial and technical support was made available in sums greater than had been previously. The development process was also institutionalised at the state level and was not simply an undertaking of private organisations, such as those concerned with the abolition of slavery in other lands (Rist 2014).

The initial concerns of the international response (perhaps best described as capital 'D' development) have remained largely in place over the last seven decades – how to achieve economic growth in order to deliver higher standards of living as well as positive development outcomes in the non-economic spheres. In the first iteration of Development policies, the focus was on enhancing economic productivity that involved large infrastructure investment and building import substitution industries. The premise of these 'modernisation' policies was that if these undeveloped countries could resemble Western (i.e. the United States) economies, they would quickly industrialise and make rapid escalations in their economic development. There were five stages to this problematic Modernisation approach. The first was the 'traditional' stage whereby the poor countries were in a state of poverty going about traditional ways of living. The second was the 'pre-take off'. Here the poor were beginning to shed their traditional modes of living for more 'modern' methods. The third stage was 'take-off' whereby the economy slowly began to gain momentum and escape the situation of poverty. Fourth was the 'drive to maturity' where the once poor societies would increasingly resemble wealthy countries with rapid industrialisation and modern economies. The final stage would be the achievement of the goal of 'mass consumption'. These five stages of growth were encapsulated by Walt Whitman Rostow (1960) whose book *The Stages of Economic Growth* was not so subtly subtitled, 'A Non-Communist Manifesto'. There was no question that Development as it was understood at that time was dependent upon the introduction of a Western capitalist system.

One of the consequences of the importance placed upon the introduction of Western capitalism as a cornerstone of the Development process was the minimisation of religion as a potential constitutive force for positive change. For Development planners, religion was understood in one of two ways. First, it was conceived as a private issue with no (or little) impact on the wider social life and could thus be ignored. Or second, it was viewed as a bottleneck to Development as it limited economic productivity through its intimate ties with other bottlenecks that included traditional economic systems or traditional relationships such as kinship, feudal or extended family ties (Clarke 2011).

The failure to appreciate religion as a potential force for positive change was not of course unexpected within the modernist discourse. Indeed, it was simply a continuation of the marginalisation of religion in Western societies that had occurred throughout the previous decades as a result of processes of secularisation (see Juergensmeyer 2010). Whilst capitalism became the overarching organising system within these newly developing countries as a result of Development programmes, its laws and mechanisms were expected to became the basis upon which to build and sustain communities. Such expectations though were not necessarily realised (Clarke 2013).

Indeed, a backlash against the Development agenda soon occurred. Capitalism through the modernist project delivered economic growth, but it also delivered great economic inequities and other market failures that worsened rather than enhanced the lives of many of the poor. Much of the backlash originated within Latin America. The basis of this backlash was analysis suggesting that increasing engagement with a capitalist world system was in fact detrimental to wellbeing and that the modern economic system worsened living standards rather than improved them. Disengagement was therefore seen to be a better policy choice than further engagement. This analysis of long-term economic data become known as Dependency theory. The clear position of this movement was that the poor were poor not because they had yet to embrace capitalism, but rather, they were poor precisely because the rich were wealthy. Poverty and affluence were two sides of the same coin and the wealth of the affluent was dependent upon the poverty of the marginalised and poor (see Gunder Frank 1967). Within this understanding, countries were not 'undeveloped' but rather were actively and purposely 'underdeveloped'. Policy prescriptions revolved around a retreat from the world capitalist system. As with Modernisation though, there was no acknowledgement that religion had any role to play or any value to add in righting the circumstances of the poor. However, at this very same time and in this very region, a second critique of modernisation, capitalism and Development was being espoused by (predominantly) Catholic theologians. Presenting a very similar concern for the marginalised, Liberation Theology sought to preference the needs of the poor based on Gospel principles of giving priority to material assistance to the most vulnerable over pious prayer (see Boff 1987 and Gutierrez 1973). Such secular and sectarian critiques though were unable to deliver sufficient practical policy alternatives and capitalism retained its dominance as the underpinning economic system in the international quest to achieve Development.

What did shift though within the Development project just prior to the turn of the twentieth century, were the policy prescriptions that were being pursued, that reflected policy shifts in so-called developed countries during the late 1970s and early 1980s. Across the developing world, policies that reduced government expenditure, privatised government assets, weakened labor laws, dismantled protectionism and generally deregulated markets were enthusiastically promoted by the World Bank and International Monetary Fund under the auspices of structural adjustment programmes. These policies were known as the Washington Consensus. As with Modernisation and Dependency though, the primary focus remained economic growth first and foremost with no consideration of religion or other aspects of culture and social practices, except as impediments to the Development process (Clarke 2011).

In recent years the international approach to achieving the Development project remains largely centred on the achievement of economic growth through a liberal capitalist market. A significant change in recent years however has been the explicit understanding that economic growth is not of itself the goal of Development, but rather there are a range of spheres that are the basis upon which Development should be assessed and that economic growth simply facilitates investment in and improvement of these spheres. This explicit widening of Development outcomes is best reflected in the Millennium Development Goals and the more recently announced Sustainable Development Goals. Within this new iteration of the Development project, non-economic spheres have been given greater prominence than previously, though the primary driver of improvement remains the achievement of economic growth.

Yet again, religious belief and religious institutions are largely excluded from this Development approach.

Running concurrently with this capital 'D' development history has been the locally situated, sub-national, community-focused interventions aimed to also improve the lives of the poor. These interventions are often facilitated by NGOs and CBOs. As these organisations have matured and professionalised over the past decades they have been responsible for raising and expending many hundreds of billions of dollars for alleviating poverty (see Watson and Clarke 2014). During this time the theory of how they successfully work with local communities has evolved and become well documented (see Ife 2013 as an example). On the whole though, the majority of these NGOs and CBOs have been relatively agnostic with regards to the role that religion plays in their own work. Certainly this is the case within most community development theory in which religion, when discussed, is largely placed within the sphere of 'culture'.

Ife (2013) sets out various principles upon which contemporary community development should be based. These principles are grouped into four main areas: foundational principles, valuing the local, having proper processes, and linking the global and local. As Ife (2013, p. 299) notes, 'these principles of community development need to be adapted, considered, reconstructed according to the context'. With regard to valuing the local these include: 1) taking into account the existing assets within local communities and the strengths and capacities that are in place, 2) valuing local knowledge on the communities themselves, 3) valuing local culture including the identity of the community, 4) valuing local resources which may include material resources or more ephemeral resources such as social networks, 5) valuing local skills and knowledge based on lived experiences of the community's own reality, and 6) valuing local processes including decision-making processes or local leaders. Religious institutions, religious leaders and religious social networks are closely intertwined within communities and cannot be separated from the day-to-day reality of these communities. The buildings owned by religious institutions are utilised by local communities, the networks of religious institutions are embedded into local communities, and religious leaders are also community-wide leaders (see McGregor et al. 2012). Excluding or failing to fully consider the role that religion plays in fulfilling these principles of community development will thereby reduce the potential impact any development interventions may have.

There remains a hesitancy to practically engage with the spiritual or religious beliefs of communities in development activities. Of course, community development work undertaken by faith-based organisations (FBOs) is the exception to this rule (Clarke and Ware 2015; Rae and Clarke 2013). Given the dominance of FBOs in many domains of community development (Jennings 2014), this exemption is significant but has not impacted widely beyond the FBO sector. Despite understanding the need to champion local culture and contextualisation of all development interventions, religion and religious institutions remain marginalised within the broader development sector. No doubt, much of this is explained by actions of past and present individuals and organisations undertaking evangelisation under the guise of development who have damaged the reputation of the development sector by these acts. Recent experiences in Aceh and Haiti following natural disasters demonstrate how religious goals of certain organisations can pollute wider humanitarian efforts. So deep-seated is this concern, that many faith-based organisations undertaking development work as expressions of their ministries are also fearful of being seen to be 'mixing' development work with evangelical activities (see Clarke 2012 for a series of case studies). This nervousness of working in the intersection of religious and development activities has the result that again the constitutive force of religion is not fully appreciated. This of course should not be taken to mean that the development activities associated with religion or religious institutions do not exist or have limited impact. That is not true. There are many examples – from all religions – where the religious imperative to improve the temporal conditions of the poor is fully realised within the best standards of community development theory (Clarke 2011). It is upon this empirical evidence base that a case begins to emerge that the nexus between religion and development is worthy of a much fuller exploration and analysis.

Religion and development nexus

Over the past decade there has been increased interest in the nexus between religion and development. Whilst still at the margins of mainstream theory and practice, the 'one-eyed giants' spoken of by Denis Goulet (1980) nearly four decades ago, who refused to acknowledge religion in the development sphere, are now slowly adjusting their vision. There has been increasing donor-funded research (such as the UK DfID funded Religions and Development research programme undertaken at the University of Birmingham, UK, the Berkley Centre for Religion, Peace and World Affairs at Georgetown University, USA, and the Knowledge Centre Religion and Development in the Netherlands), research publications (see Clarke 2011, Deneulin and Bano 2009, ter Haar 2011, Rees 2011, Fountain et al. 2015) and reflection on religion and development practices (see case studies in Clarke 2013). There has also been an increase in the public advocacy of religious institutions around certain development issues. For example, the global Jubilee 2000 and the subsequent Make Poverty History campaigns had religious geneses. Religion has also become increasingly visible in the public sphere and important in terms of civic culture as described in the Introduction. Further, the process of globalisation has led to increased religious diversity and enhanced the reach of religion. Religious groups are able to connect across the globe in ways that were not possible until only recently, resulting in a stronger sense of identity and wielding a greater sense of influence. Through all of this, it has become increasingly difficult to continue shutting out or ignoring the intersection between religion and development.

Of course, religion is not the 'answer' to the world's woes. Achieving the goals associated with development cannot be left to religious fervour or dedication.

Suggesting such positions is without merit. Indeed, there are many development problems that have either their roots in religious belief systems or practices or at least are exacerbated by religious belief systems and practices. Cogent arguments can be made that religion has contributed to many of the issues that bolster poverty, including gender inequity, the doctrine of predestination, religious spending on temples, emphasis on non-temporal salvation, protecting vested interests of those in authority, etc. It is important to note the negative impact of religion on world conflict (Fox and Sandler 2006), security issues (Seiple and Hoover 2004), and extremism in international politics (Haynes 2007; Juergensmeyer 2008). Such critiques should not be ignored. But nor should these failures be allowed to be considered the sole impact of religion and religious institutions on global temporal affairs.

As a majority of the world's population professes religious belief, there can be no doubt that religion is part of their lived experience. Religious beliefs do affect how people view the world and their place in it. Engaging with religious people and institutions can therefore provide multiple platforms upon which successful development interventions are likely to be sustained and effective. Engaging with religious groups and institutions however needs to be authentic if it is to be successful. Authentic engagement with religion does not require there to be shared religious beliefs or even the holding of religious faith by those working within the development sector. What is required though is an understanding that the religious beliefs held by those individuals and communities in need of assistance do affect their worldviews and responses to their own lived experiences. Such authentic engagement remains uncommon within the development sector. As discussed, the secularisation of the development process has meant that religion has long been excluded from mainstream discussions of international development. Whilst this is slowly changing, the argument that religion should not be seen as something *apart* from development processes, but rather it should be seen as *a part* of these processes has yet to be fully incorporated into best practice.

'Normalising' religion into development theory and practice is an ongoing enterprise. While great strides have been made in recent years, the power of the religious and development nexus remains underutilised and not greatly understood. Nearly 40 years ago, Goulet (1980, p. 485) made the case for harnessing the power of religion for the cause of development:

> [Religious beliefs]… harbour within them a latent dynamism which, when properly respected, can serve as the springboard for modes of development which are more humane than those drawn from outside paradigms. When development builds from indigenous values it extracts lower social costs and imposes less human suffering and cultural destruction than when it copies outside models. This is so because indigenously-rooted values are the matrix whence people derive meaning in their lives, a sense of identity and cultural integrity, and the experience of continuity with their environment and their past even in the midst of change.

Underscoring Goulet's argument though is the need not to simply pay lip service to religious belief or institutions by simply using religious rhetoric to 'sell' development interventions, but rather to engage deeply with local values and traditions. Such engagement will therefore move beyond simply presenting interventions in religious language, colours or flavours but rather draw on the existing community values to shape local development goals in the first instance. Drawing deeply on these existing values and narratives will result in development goals that are relevant and appropriate to existing needs and which will resonate with the local population. Local values therefore provide a dynamism that supports new and innovative ways to approach development. An authentic engagement with the affected communities will necessarily be more effective than interventions that are unauthentic and simply presented in local 'religious dress'.

Better understanding how religion and development intersect will enhance the ability of community development interventions to improve wellbeing. For much of its modern history, religion has either been ignored or treated with hostility within development theory and practice. Given the secular history of the modern development project – flowing out of the Enlightenment – such a position on religion is not unexpected. However, given the overwhelming majority of the world's population self-report as holding religious belief and the impact these beliefs have on people's worldview, authentic engagement with religion by the development sector is well overdue. Indeed, in recent years there has been increased interest in both theory and practice, but more work is required. Of course, such engagement is not simply one-directional. Where religious beliefs, practices and leadership do work against good change and freedom, then it is incumbent upon the development sector to challenge these and seek better outcomes for the most vulnerable. Such dialogue though will be more effective if there is increased religious literacy and a track record of engagement between religious and non-religious organisations.

As will be explored in this volume, there are many instances where development activities are being undertaken in religious locations. Such merging of sacred place and development space is not an exception to practice but a daily occurrence across the globe that is yet to be fully appreciated. The case studies explored in this volume will hopefully add to the increasing empirical evidence base of the importance of understanding better the religion development nexus and how this intersection can be a positive force for good change and enhanced wellbeing. They will also draw upon insights gained from literature on space, place and religion from the geographical discipline, which have yet to be applied to development studies in detail and are explored below.

Geography and religion

Lily Kong (1990, 2001, 2010)[2] has mapped the development of geographical research on religion over three decades. Kong (2010) explains how the events of 11 September 2001 and terrorist attacks in Bali, Madrid, London and Mumbai in the 2000s stimulated interest in this field, as has the rise of religious diversity in many nations due to increased migration. This has led, as Jürgen Habermas (2006, 2008) notably observed and as has been described in detail in the Introduction, to religion playing more of a prominent role in the public sphere at the turn of the twentieth century and to a growth of research on 'post-secular' societies, including by some geographers of religion.

Kong (1990, p. 356) examined the origins of geographical research on religion in her first review article, stating that while Greek geographers' world maps and diagrams reflected a world shaped by religious principles including 'spatial order' these were in fact examples of what Erich Isaac (1965) referred to as 'religious geography' rather than an early 'geography of religion'. By the sixteenth century an 'ecclesiastical geography' emerged with the mapping of Christianity's global spatial advance (Kong 1990, p. 365 citing Isaac 1965, p. 356). At the same time a 'historical geography of biblical times' attempted to identify and locate places named and/or referred to in The Bible illustrating the power of Christianity (Isaac 1965, p. 8 quoted in Kong 1990, p. 357).

From the late seventeenth until the nineteenth century a 'physicotheological stance' arose in which scholars argued that evidence of God's wisdom could be found in nature given its capacity to support life (Kong 1990, p. 357 citing Glacken 1956, 1967, 1980). Geographers also began to explore how religions were affected by the places in which they arose, and how this impacted on what was sacred to them and also their views of what happened after death (Kong 1990).[3] Weber however inverted these environmentally deterministic models by calling for the study of religion's impact on society and economics, which later was extended by other scholars to the study of religion's influence on the environment (Kong 1990). As Isaac (1959–1960 quoted in Kong 1990, p. 358) stated: 'the geography of religion is the study of the part played by the religious motive in man's transformation of the landscape'. Kong (1990, p. 358) explains that while this approach is still used, it has been widely criticised and that contemporary studies focus more on 'reciprocity in the network of relations' between religion, environment and society.

Research on cultural geography and religion from the 1960s to the 1990s explored the spatial growth and decline, and also the distribution of religious groups over time, the impact that religious groups have had on landscapes through the creation of sacred structures and monuments, and also religious pilgrimages. These studies examined how the symbolic meanings of places are changeable, how religious symbolism can be used for political ends, how tensions can arise between religious groups, and/or religious and secular uses of land, and the power relations between these groups, particularly in increasingly plural societies. They also examined the impact religion has had on shaping attitudes to nature and animal life and the role of religion in causing and ameliorating environmental risks and crises (Kong 1990).[4] Kong (1990) concluded her first review article by lamenting that most of these studies focused on institutionalised religious systems, reflecting a Western Christian bias when it came to understanding religions.

Many of these trends have continued in later geographical studies of religion, which Kong (2001, p. 211) believes to be centred around key themes of 'the politics and poetics of religious place, identity and community'. In her second review article, Kong (2001, p. 226) explained that there was a need to research sites 'beyond the "officially sacred"' churches, temples, and mosques such as 'indigenous sacred sites, religious schools, religious organisations and their premises (communal halls), pilgrimage routes (apart from the sites themselves), religious objects, memorials and roadside shrines, domestic shrines, and religious processions and festivals'. She also called for further exploration of 'sensuous sacred geographies', shifting the focus of research from the 'visual and kinetic to aural/audio experiences and constructions of the sacred'. By 2010, Kong reported that there had certainly been an increase of research on everyday religious places and places, including sites listed above and also of homes, banking and financial institutions, and media spaces.[5] Kim Knott's (2005, p. 2) research is a notable example of this shift focused on *The Location of Religion* in 'contemporary everyday spaces,' as are Shampa Mazumdar and Sanjoy Mazumdar's (2009, 2012) studies on immigrant homes and home gardens. Their research has demonstrated that 'there are many ways in which everyday spaces can be implicated in religious meaning-making, legitimating, maintaining and enhancing, but also challenging religious life, beliefs, practices and identities' (Kong 2010, p. 757). However, Kong (2010) states that there is still a need to further explore embodied and sensuous experiences of the sacred.

Kong (2001, p. 226) also highlighted the need for more 'historical and place-specific analysis' of religion and for various different scales of analysis examining the body, local, regional, national and global developments. She also emphasised that religious places hold different meanings for different constitutions of the population depending for example on their gender, age, minority or majority position (Kong 2001). By 2010, Kong (2010) described how there has been a growing emphasis on research on the religious identity construction of minority youth and on gender and religion, largely focused on Islam and Muslims, among geographers. Research on religion and human mobility has also burgeoned with particular emphasis on the ways in which processes of colonisation and migration have shaped and are shaping religious landscapes of sending and receiving countries, diasporic religious identities and transnational networks and ties. These developments are also increasingly considered with regard to the impact on domestic politics, identity and citizenship, and again largely centred on Islam and Muslim communities (Kong 2010).[6] Kong (2010, p. 762) notes that the relative neglect of research on other religious groups, including new religions, and those with beliefs outside of official 'world religions' continues to be 'disappointing'.

In 2001, Kong (2001, p. 212) also observed that 'the intersection of sacred and secular forces in the making of place' also needs to be more fully acknowledged in geographical inquiry for,

> while the sacred is often constructed, and gathers meaning in opposition to the secular, place is often multivalent, and requires an acknowledgement of

> simultaneous, fluctuating and conflicting investment of sacred and secular meanings in any one site.
>
> (Kong 2001, p. 212)

Kong (2010, p. 765) is sceptical of the assertion that we are experiencing a re-emergence of religion at the turn of the twenty-first century and of applying the term postsecularisation in 'a globalizing and totalizing way'. Instead she posits that perhaps 'an abiding spirituality... has persisted in the face of modernity' and that we must be mindful that 'the force of religion in everyday lives today in geographically contingent situations may be different.' Kong (2010, p. 765) further argues that geographers must investigate the role of religions and faith-based organisations in creating and addressing social inequality and environmental issues. She proposes four global issues, which are included in the UN Millennium Development Goals, that require further investigation regarding the intersection of the sacred and the secular in contemporary societies: 'rapid urbanization and social inequality; a deteriorating environment; an ageing population; and increasing human mobilities'.

Kong (2001) also stressed the importance of understanding religion's role in moral geography and the way in which religious and secular constructions of morality and justice are played out in space. Her 2001 article focused largely on the politics and poetics of space, which are particularly relevant to the case studies included in this volume on sacred places as development spaces. The following sections explore the work of scholars cited by Kong, and her observations in more detail.

The politics and poetics of space

According to David Chidester and Edward T. Linenthal (1995, p. 5) definitions of the sacred can be categorised as 'substantial' or 'situational'. Substantial definitions, such as Gerardus van der Leeuw's (1938) 'power', Rudolph Otto's (1950) 'holy', or Mircea Eliade's 'real' (1961), describe the 'essential character' of the sacred as 'an uncanny, awesome, or powerful manifestation of reality, full of ultimate significance' (Chidester and Linenthal 1995, p. 5), focusing on the 'experiential, imaginative, and poetic dynamics of sacred space' (Chidester and Linenthal 1995, p. 32). As Belden C. Lane (2002, p. 21) stated, drawing on Eliade, 'place may be itself possessed of power and life' and its sacredness revealed to humans.

Situational definitions, beginning with Emile Durkheim, by contrast locate the sacred in the social, arguing that 'nothing is inherently sacred' and that the sacred is 'an empty signifier' (Chidester and Linenthal 1995, p. 5–6). Claude Lévi-Strauss (1950 quoted in Chidester and Linenthal 1995, p. 6) stated that the sacred is 'a value of indeterminate signification, in itself empty of meaning and therefore susceptible to the reception of any meaning whatsoever'. Chidester and Linenthal (1995, p. 6) further explained:

> As a situational term, therefore, the sacred is nothing more nor less than a notional supplement to the ongoing cultural work of sacralizing space,

> time, persons, and social relations. Situational, relational, and frequently, if not inherently, contested, the sacred is a by-product of this work of sacralization.

Chidester and Linenthal (1995, p. 6) likened substantial and situational approaches with what they called 'the poetics and the politics of sacred space'. According to van der Leeuw (1938 cited in Chidester and Linenthal 1995, p. 7), sacred places of home, temple, settlement, pilgrimage site, and human body 'formed a recursive series of metaphoric equivalences', where for example 'home was a temple, temple a home'.

Van der Leeuw's (1938 cited in Chidester and Linenthal 1995, p. 7–8), work was however also concerned with a politics of sacred space, where establishment of sacred place was recognised as a conquest of space and where places were powerful not just because they were meaningful but because they had been appropriated, and were owned. This 'politics of property' 'linked power, possibility, and property as forces in the production of sacred space' (p. 8). Moreover, according to van der Leeuw the sanctity of sacred places involved a 'politics of exclusion' (p. 8) as it was maintained by keeping, leaving and forcing some people out. Michel Foucault (quoted in Rabinow 1984, p. 252) similarly observed a 'problem of a monastery as xenophobic' given the 'precise regulations concerning life in common; affecting sleeping, eating, prayer' and 'the place of each individual in all of that'.

Moreover, van der Leeuw (1938, pp. 395–396 cited and quoted in Chidester and Linenthal 1995, p. 9) positioned modern people as 'political exiles from the sacred' and unable to realise the 'unitary power' that was readily experienced in pre-modern societies. Lane (2002) also explained how many indigenous and pagan cultures believe that the earth and the cosmos are inherently sacred spaces and places and that, as Eliade argued, it was Judeo-Christian prophets and later missionaries that disrupted these worldviews. Modernity and processes of secularisation further led to the 'disenchantment' of the world (Weber quoted in Lane 2002, p. 22). Lane (2002, p. 23) stated that as a result, 'God has been removed from the particularity of place, extracted from the natural environment'.

Chidester and Linenthal (1995, p. 9) observed that paying attention to 'the politics of position and property, exclusion and exile' provided 'new ways of understanding how specific sites and environments, geographical relations and symbolic orientations, can be produced and reproduced as sacred space'. In their own study of sacred spaces in Hawai'i, they described how 'ritualization, reinterpretation, and contests over legitimate ownership' also play an important role in 'the production of sacred space'. Ritualisation can be understood as an 'embodied spacial practice' where ritual acts such as ceremonies, prayer, and pilgrimage are 'formalized, repeatable symbolic performances' that 'consecrate sacred space'. Ritual is therefore 'a defining feature of sacralization' (pp. 9–10). Sacred places, Lane (2002, p. 25) similarly noted are often 'ordinary' places, 'ritually set apart to become extraordinary'. Drawing on Pierre Bourdieu (1977 cited in Chidester and Linenthal 1995, p. 10), Chidester and Linenthal explained how embodied practices produce and reproduce ritualised habitus 'as a dynamic special ordering of knowledge and power' and how they can both consecrate and also desecrate sacred places. As geographer David Harvey (1989, p. 214, quoted in Chidester and Linenthal 1995, p. 12) stated: 'Symbolic orderings of space and time provide a framework for experience through which we learn who or what we are in society.' They define who is to be venerated, and who is excluded and denigrated, distinguishing 'center from periphery, inside from outside' (Chidester and Linenthal 1995, p. 12).

Sacred built places of worship, including temples, synagogues, mosques and churches are 'ritualized' and distinguished as 'cultural locations of religious meaning and significance' (Chidester and Linenthal 1995, p. 13) as are other sacred places such as homes, cemeteries, tourist attractions and shopping centres.[7] These sacred places can function as 'nodal points' within different spatial networks (Soja 1989, pp. 149, 151 quoted in Chidester and Linenthal 1995, p. 13). Chidester and Linenthal (1995, p. 14–15) noted that 'religious worldviews embody broader spatial orientations that locate human beings in a meaningful, powerful world' and that 'attention to geographical relations between center and periphery locates specific sacred sites or environments within a larger network of political, social, economic, and symbolic relations of power', often intersecting with class, race, ethnicity and gender.

As Chidester and Linenthal (1995, p. 16) observed:

> Sacred space may be set apart, but not in the absolute, heterogeneous sense that Eliade insisted upon. Against all the efforts of religious actors, sacred space is inevitably entangled with the entrepreneurial, the social, the political, and other 'profane' forces. In fact, ... a space or place is often experienced as most sacred by those who perceive it at risk of being desecrated by the very forces – economic, social, and political – that made its consecration possible in the first place.

Natural environments are also frequently described as sacred spaces, in both substantial and situational senses. Space itself, and natural landscapes are viewed by some with awe and wonder, akin to the 'power', the 'real' that permeates the Universe, believing they are made and shaped by supernatural forces (Chidester and Linenthal 1995). While others argue that 'nature, in its human meaning and significance, is a cultural product' (Chidester and Linenthal 1995, p. 13) and that natural spaces too are sites of contestation and political struggle.

As Chidester and Linenthal (1995, p. 15) explained, 'a sacred space is not merely discovered, or founded, or constructed; it is claimed, owned, and operated by people advancing specific interests.' They stated:

> Sacred places are arenas in which power relations can be reinforced, in which relations between insiders and outsiders, rulers and subjects, elders and juniors, males and females, and so on, can be adjudicated. But those power relations are always resisted.
>
> (Chidester and Linenthal 1995, p. 16)

Sacred places, therefore, have 'the potential of being as disruptive' as they are 'integrative' (Lane 2002, p. 48).

Chidester and Linenthal (1995) argued that sacred space is contested primarily for two reasons. First, because it is spatial and that as John Urry (1985, p. 30 quoted in Chidester and Linenthal 1995, p. 18) stated 'space is necessarily limited and there has to be competition and conflict over its organization and control'. And second, given that sacred place can 'signify almost anything' and mean many different things to different people and groups, it 'is not defined by spatial limits' but rather is 'open to unlimited claims and counter claims on its significance'. Consequently, conflicts arise 'not only over scarce resources but also over symbolic surpluses that are abundantly available for appropriation'. They concluded:

> Through appropriation and exclusion, inversion and hybridization, sacred space is produced and reproduced. Relational, situational, and contested, sacred places are necessarily located within these conflictual strategies of symbolic engagement.
>
> (Chidester and Linenthal 1995, p. 20)

Foucault (quoted in Rabinow 1984) also provided significant insights on space, power and contestation. He explained how in the eighteenth century state documents contained considerable reflection on architecture and the planning of cities 'as a function of the aims and techniques of the government of societies' (p. 239), alongside other elements of governmental rationality, which sought to penetrate and regulate them. Urban spaces exacerbated risks of disease and revolution in nineteenth-century Europe and fast expanding railroad systems enhanced mobility and established new networks for communication. However, despite hopes that the railways would lead to the creation of more peaceful societies, they made wars easier to fight.

Foucault (quoted in Rabinow 1984, p. 246) stated that 'it can never be inherent in the structure of things to guarantee the exercise of freedom' as '[l]iberty is a *practice*' that 'must be exercised'. No one thing or project is totally oppressive or liberating. He elucidated 'no matter how terrifying a given system may be, there always remain the possibilities of resistance, disobedience, and oppositional groupings' (p. 245). At the same time, despite the best intentions of projects that aim to modify or break constraints, none can assure that liberty will be established by these projects themselves. Architecture, for example, can only resolve social issues 'when the liberating intentions of the architect coincide with the real practice of the people in the exercise of their freedom' (p. 246). Foucault (quoted in Rabinow 1984, p. 246) declared:

> I think it is somewhat arbitrary to try to dissociate the effective practice of freedom by people, the practice of social relations, and the spatial distributions in which they find themselves. If they are separated, they become impossible to understand. Each can only be understood through the other.

Foucault (quoted in Rabinow 1984, p. 247) further explained that 'the exercise of freedom… can only function when there is a certain convergence; in the case of divergence or distortion, it immediately becomes the opposite of that which had been intended… There are only reciprocal relations, and the perpetual gaps between intentions in relation to one another.' He also stated that: 'Space is fundamental in any form of communal life; space is fundamental in any exercise of power' (p. 252). Foucault (1984) argued that while new building techniques, for example, can influence human relations, these techniques cannot be invented and applied without human relations that influence their development. 'What is interesting', said Foucault (quoted in Rabinow 1984, p. 254), 'is always interconnection, not the primacy of this over that, which never has any meaning'.

Examples of contemporary theories of spaces of resistance, are Homi K. Bhabha (1994) and Edward Soja's (1996) notions of 'third space', which have recently been applied to studies of digital activism. Bhabha (1990, p. 211) likened cultural hybridity to third space explaining that 'it displaces the histories that constitute it, and sets up new structures of authority, new political initiatives, which are inadequately understood through received wisdom' creating 'a new area of negotiation of meaning and representation'. Hybridity 'bears the traces of those feelings and practices which inform it, just like a translation, so that hybridity puts together the traces of certain other meanings or discourses'. Stewart M. Hoover and Nabil Echchaibi (2012, pp. 3, 5) explain how digital 'third places' or 'third spaces' 'describe something alternative to other, prior, or dominant domains' and how 'the digital might support the creation or maintenance of physical third spaces, most commonly in relation to the project of enhancing civic engagement' (2012, pp. 6–8). Recently, Emma Tomalin, Caroline Starkey and Anna Halafoff (2015) have argued that the Buddhist women's social movement comprises an offline and online 'third space', in which a community of women and men, drawing upon traditional and modern narratives and technologies, share a focus on highlighting and improving women's opportunities for practice and recognition within Buddhism. Online 'third spaces', they argue, have been created to complement real world activities, which question and usurp dominant patriarchal narratives within Buddhism.

In 2010, Kong (2010, p. 757) concluded that there were a growing number of studies on the politics of space focused largely on mosques in non-Muslim countries, which demonstrate that 'despite the official rhetoric of multiculturalism in many cities, sacred spaces are often at the heart of intense contestation, with wider community resistances to the establishment of "unfamiliar" religious sites or sacred sites of minority groups'. The Buddhist women's social movement also continues to meet with considerable resistance from patriarchal Buddhist authorities, which will be discussed in more detail in Chapter 4. Kong (2001, p. 227) also underscored the need to interrogate different dialectics within scholarship on religion and geography 'of public and private, politics and poetics, social and spatial' at the theoretical level. Finally, it is important to note that Kong (2001) stressed the connections between and interrelationships of politics and poetics, the situational and the substantial, private and public, religious and secular, when examining sacred places and spaces.

Indeed, Peter Hopkins, Kong and Elizabeth Olson's (2013) recent edited collection focuses on the 'co-production of religion and place across a range of contexts, scales, and networks'. Harvey (2004) has also offered a tripartite model of space comprising absolute space, relative space and relational space. Harvey proposed that space can be one or all of these components at any time, depending on context. Human practices create and shape space, and the three elements coexist in a dialectical interplay. He cited Ground Zero, in New York City, as an example of a space which is at once absolute, relative, and relational; it is a 'physical and legal entity' situated in absolute space; flows of people, culture and capital maintain it is a 'living habitat', and interaction with the processes of economic globalisation, climate change, history, and collective memories – particularly of traumatic events – construct it as a relational space (p. 6). Harvey (2004, p. 4) stated: 'An event or a thing at a point in space cannot be understood by appeal to what exists only at that point. It depends upon everything else going on around it.'

Mazumdar and Mazumdar (2009, p. 265) similarly observed '"an ecology of religion" suggesting a strong link between home spaces, landscapes, and ritual'. They further explain how that at this time of 'heightened religious tension' it is important to examine how everyday sacred places 'through decor, aesthetics, and landscaping, can inculcate tranquility, inner peace, religiosity, and spirituality'. Moreover, their research indicates that:

> When mixed with sacredness, everyday activities, such as tending to the garden, cleaning the pond, raking leaves, pruning bushes, and even taking a leisurely walk along a meandering garden path can be psychologically calming and reflective.
>
> (Mazumdar and Mazumdar 2009, p. 265)

Health geographical literature on 'therapeutic landscapes' emerged in the 1990s and has expanded its focus in the 2000s beyond investigation of places with 'a reputation for healing' to those that more broadly focused on promoting well-being and maintaining health, in more formal health care settings and 'everyday geographies of care' (Gesler 2005, pp. 295–296). Ideas of therapeutic landscape are 'context dependent' and variable over time and between individuals (p. 297). 'What may be healing for one individual or group', explained Allison M. Williams (2007, pp. 2–3), 'may not be for another' and is also 'affected by local social and economic conditions and their associated change'. Williams (2007, p. 10) has also called for more research into therapeutic landscapes and spiritual wellbeing, including at spiritually reputed sites such as shrines and sacred places, and also in 'geographies of health care, health promotion, and everyday and imagined geographies'. Indeed, the pressures of modernity and capitalism have led to a rise of interest in, and scholarly research on, spiritual and religious practices such as meditation, mindfulness, yoga and retreats, that enable repose from the relentless pace of ultramodern life and spiritual technologies for managing stress and living sustainable ethical lives (Conradson 2007; Hoyez 2007).

Another notable publication that aims for a more holistic study of sacred places is Lane's (2002) *Landscapes of the Sacred*. The first 1988 edition was centred on 'the individual human appropriation of sacred places', focusing on 'the spiritualized significance' that people had attributed to places rather than on the cultural and phenomenological aspects of place. In the revised version Lane remained highly influenced by Eliade and convinced of the power of stories in 'the enduring identity of sacred place.' Yet he also flagged the risks of 'an individualized (even ideological) appropriation of place narratives that quickly strips them of their cultural and material roots in order to serve larger spiritual (or didactic) ends' (Lane 2002, p. ix). Lane (2002, p. 5) further stated that those who focus on the autonomous and magical qualities of place 'too easily disregard the social, economic, and political forces that inevitably determine negotiations about their use'.

That being said, Lane (2002, p. x) still argued 'that the role of the storyteller is essential in grasping the power that place exerts on the religious imagination' as '[w]e never exhaust the mystery of a devotional site by simply unraveling the cultural threads from which it is woven... The religious perspective of those who perceive a place as sacred is certainly a constitutive part of their seeing'. Lane (2002, p. xi) poetically recounted how places have 'mediated the holy for [him]'. His can therefore be described as both a substantial and situational study of sacred landscapes, urban and rural, built and natural.

'Identifying the sacred character of a place', wrote Lane (2002, p. 3) 'involves much more than gathering the random accounts of its individual spiritual encounters, significant as these may be.' It also involves examining 'a whole history of cultural tensions and conflicting claims, even ecological shifts in the terrain itself' as sacred places 'generate political polarities' as does 'the practice of any authentic spirituality' (p. 4). Lane (2002, p. 4) added that a sacred place 'is necessarily more than a construction of the human imagination', and noted that,

> sacred places also participate in the entire array of sensory exchanges that play across the land, reaching far beyond the impact of human influence alone. The motion of wind through the limbs of a juniper tree in a red rock canyon, the long-tailed magpie that leaves seeds of a distant wildflower in its droppings beside a small arroyo, the shifting of rock in a fissure caused by water erosion – these, too, are a part of the dynamic reciprocity that makes up the ambient character of any desert monastery or roadside shrine.
>
> (Lane 2002, p. 4)

The 'stories most people tell of their own experiences of place as "sacred"' recounted Lane (2002, p. 41), 'almost inevitably honor the participation of the whole environment.' Whereas, he stated, a more situational social constructivist approach, 'fails to recognize place itself as a participant in the formation of that experience' (p. 44). By contrast, Lane explained that phenomenological approaches highlight the 'reciprocity' and 'intersubjectivity that exists between the human and more-than-human world, stressing the importance of embodiment in the human experience of place' (p. 44). Lane argued what was needed was a more complete 'multidimensional understanding' of the 'diverse character' and 'functions' of particular places (pp. 44–45).

Lane (2002, p. 11) also raised the challenge of finding language to adequately describe spiritual experiences of place and proposed the 'poetic language of metaphor and suggestion' as perhaps the most effective medium. Lane's work evokes a poetic re-enchantment of place, and attempts to balance this at least in part with a critical situational inquiry.

Conclusion

This volume will attempt a similar, yet reverse approach, focusing more on the social and political construction of places as development spaces, yet also including and genuinely hearing participants' stories of the diverse ways in which their belief systems have and continue to influence their experiences of the places in which they locate their development activities. We will also allow for the places to speak for themselves through our, the authors', descriptions of them and we will also record and analyse the reciprocal embodied relationships we have observed between sacred places, both natural and built, actors who design and conduct development programmes and those participating in them.

We will draw on and apply religion and development literature and geographical studies of religion described above to our case studies in order to further contribute to a multidimensional understanding of religion, place and space that focuses primarily on development activities. We will investigate local and global partnerships and networks that bridge sacred and secular divides. We will also examine both the poetics and politics of sacred places, drawing heavily on the stories we have gathered from our participants and our own observations of their development projects. In so doing we aim to assist those working in the field of religion and development to pay closer attention to the importance of place when designing, conducting and participating in development activities in partnership with local actors, given the context specificity of such projects and significance of places. Finally, we will contribute to the growing body of literature on religion and place, and add new insights pertaining to sacred places and sustainable development spaces.

Notes

1 See also Alolo and Connell (2013), Fang and Bi (2013), and Miller (2013) for descriptions of how traditional African religion, Confucianism and Daoism respectively all require adherents to seek to positively impact the wellbeing of others in need.

2 Kong (1990, 2001, 2010) cites numerous authors in her articles who have conducted geographical research on religion. We have for the most part summarised Kong's analysis of her field in this chapter so for more detailed information on the studies that she has cited please refer to her articles. We have included citations where she has quoted material or referred specifically to another author's theory or observation.

3 See Kong (1990) for examples of these early studies.
4 See Kong (1990) for examples of these studies.
5 See Kong (2010) for examples of these studies.
6 See Kong (2010) for examples of these studies.
7 See Chidester and Linenthal (1995, p. 13) for examples of studies investigating these sites of sacred significance in America.

References

Alolo, N. & Connell, J. 2013, 'Indigenous religions and development: African traditional religions', in M. Clarke (ed.), *Handbook of research on religion and development*, Edward Elgar, Cheltenham, pp. 138–163.

Bhabha, H.K. 1994, *The location of culture*, Routledge, London.

Bhabha, H.K. 1990, 'The third space: Interview with Homi Bhabha', in J. Rutherford (ed.), *Identity: Community, culture, difference*, Lawrence and Wishart, London, pp. 207–221.

Boff, L. 1987, *Introducing liberation theology*, Orbis Books, Maryknoll.

Bourdieu, P. 1977, *Outline of a theory of practice*, trans. R. Nice, Cambridge University Press, Cambridge, original work published 1972.

Büttner, M. 1980, 'On the history and philosophy of the geography of religion in Germany', *Religion*, vol. 10, no. 1, pp. 86–119.

Chambers, R. 1983, *Rural development: Putting the last first*, Longman, Harlow.

Chambers, R. 2005, *Ideas for development*, Earthscan, London.

Chidester, D. & Linenthal, E.T. 1995, 'Introduction', in D. Chidester & E.T. Linenthal (eds.), *American sacred space*, Indiana University Press, Bloomington, pp. 1–42.

Clarke, M. 2011, *Development and religion: Theology and practice*, Edward ElgarCheltenham.

Clarke, M. (ed.) 2012, *Mission and development: God's work or good works?* Continuum Books, London.

Clarke, M. (ed.) 2013, *Handbook of research on development and religion*, Edward Elgar, Cheltenham.

Clarke, M., Feeny, S., & Donnelly, J. 2014, 'Water, sanitation and hygiene interventions in the Pacific: Defining, assessing and improving "Sustainability"', *European Journal of Development Research*, vol. 26, no. 5, pp. 692–706.

Clarke, M. & Ware, V. 2015, 'Understanding faith-based organisations: How FBOs are contrasted with NGOs in international development literature', *Progress in Development Studies*, vol. 15, no. 1, pp. 37–48.

Conradson 2007, 'The experiential economy of stillness: Places of retreat in contemporary Britain', in A.M. Williams (ed), *Therapeutic Landscapes*, Ashgate, Aldershot, pp. 33–48.

Craig, D. & Porter, D. 1997, 'Framing participation: Development projects, professionals, and organizations', *Development in Practice*, vol. 7, no. 3, pp. 229–236.

Deneulin, S. & Bano, M. 2009, *Religion in development: Rewriting the secular script*, Zed Books, London.

Eliade, M. 1961, *Sacred and profane*, trans. W.R. Tiask, Harcourt, Brace, New York, original work published 1957.

Fang, X. & Bi, L. 2013, 'Confucianism', in M. Clarke (ed.), *Handbook of research on religion and development*, Edward Elgar, Cheltenham.

Fountain, P., Bush, R. & Feener, R. (eds.) 2015, *Religion and the politics of development*, Palgrave Macmillan, Basingstoke.

Fox, J. & Sandler, S. (eds.) 2006, *Religion in world conflict*, Routledge, London.

Gesler, W. 2005, 'Editorial, therapeutic lansdscapes: An emmerging theme', *Health & Place*, vol. 11, no. 4, pp. 295–297.

Glacken, C.J. 1956, 'Changing ideas of the habitable world', in W.L. Thomas, Jr (ed.), *Man's role in changing the face of the earth*, University of Chicago Press, Chicago, pp. 70–92.

Glacken, C.J. 1967, *Traces on the Rhodian shore*, University of California Press, Berkeley.

Goulet, D. 1980, 'Development experts: The one-eyed giants', *World Development*, vol. 8, nos. 6–7, pp. 481–489.

Gunder Frank, A. 1967, *Capitalism and underdevelopment in Latin America*, Monthly Review Press, New York.

Gutierrez, G. 1973, *A theology of liberation*, Orbis Books, Maryknoll.

Habermas, J. 2006, 'Religion in the public sphere', *European Journal of Philosophy*, vol. 14, no. 1, pp. 1–25.

Habermas, J. 2008, 'Notes on a post-secular society', sightandsound.com, 18 June 2008, viewed 10 February 2015, http://www.signandsight.com/features/1714.html.

Harvey, D. 1989, *The condition of postmodernity: An enquiry into the origins of cultural change*, Blackwell, Oxford.

Harvey, D. 2004, 'Space as a key word', paper for Marx and Philosophy Conference, 29 May 2004, Institute of Education, London.

Haynes, J. 2007, *An introduction to international relations and religion*, Pearson and Longman, Harlow.

Hoover, S.M. & Echchaibi, N. 2012, *The 'third space' of digital religion*, viewed 4 July 2014, http://cmrc.colorado.edu/wp-content/uploads/2012/03/Third-Spaces-Essay-Draft-Final.pdf

Hopkins, P., Kong, L. & Olson, E. 2013, *Religion and space: Landscape, politics and peity*, Springer, Dordrecht.

Hoyez, A. 2007, 'From Rishikesh to Yogaville: The globalization of therapeutic landscapes,' in A.M. Williams (ed.), *Therapeutic landscapes*, Ashgate, Aldershot. pp. 49–64.

Ife, J. 2013, *Community development in an uncertain world*, Cambridge University Press, Cambridge.

Isaac, E. 1959–60, 'Religion, landscape and space,' *Landscape*, vol. 9, no. 2, pp. 14–18.

Isaac, E. 1965, *Religious geography and the geography of religion*, in Man and the Earth, University of Colorado Studies, Series in Earth Sciences No. 3, University of Colorado Press, Boulder.

Jennings, M. 2014 'Bridging the local and the global: Faith-based organisations as non-state providers in Tanzania', in M. Cammett & L.M. MacLean (eds.), *The politics of non-state social welfare*, Cornell University Press, Ithaca, pp. 119–136.

Juergensmeyer, M. 2008, *Global rebellion: Religious challenges to the secular state, from Christian militias to Al Qaeda*, University of California Press, Berkeley.

Juergensmeyer, M. 2010, 'The global rise of religious nationalism', *Australian Journal of International Affairs*, vol. 64, no. 3, pp. 262–273.

Kingsbury, D., McKay, J., Hunt, J., McGillivray, M. & Clarke, M. 2011, *International development*, Palgrave-MacMillian, London.

Knott, K. 2005, *The location of religion: A spatial analysis*, Equinox, London.

Kong, L. 1990, 'Geography and religion: Trends and prospects', *Progress in Human Geography*, vol. 14, no. 3, pp. 355–371.

Kong, L. 2001, 'Mapping "new" geographies of religion: Politics and poetics in modernity', *Progress in Human Geography*, vol. 25, no. 2, pp. 211–233.

Kong, L. 2010, 'Global shifts, theoretical shifts: Changing geographies of religion', *Progress in Human Geography*, vol. 34, no. 6, pp. 755–776.

Lane, B.C. 2002, *Landscapes of the sacred: Geography and narrative in American spirituality (expanded edition)*, The John Hopkins University Press, Baltimore and London.

Levi-Strauss, C. 1950, 'Introduction à l'œuvre de Marcel Mauss', in M. Mauss, *Sociologie et anthropologie*, Presses universitaires de France, Paris.

Mazumdar, S. & Mazumdar, S. 2012, 'Immigrant home gardens: Places of religion, culture, ecology, and family', *Landscape and Urban Planning*, vol. 105, no. 3, pp. 258–265.

Mazumdar, S. & Mazumdar, S. 2009, 'Religion, immigration, and home making in diaspora: Hindu space in Southern California', *Journal of Environmental Psychology*, vol. 29, no. 2, pp. 256–266.

McGillivray, M. 2012, 'What is development', in D. Kingsbury, J. McKay, J. Hunt, M. McGillivray & M. Clarke, *International development, issues and challenges*, Palgrave, London, pp. 23–52.

McGregor, A., Skeaff, A., & Bevan, M. 2012, 'Overcoming secularism? Catholic development geographies in Timor-Leste,' *Third World Quarterly*, vol. 33, no. 6, pp. 1129–1146.

Miller, J. 2013, 'Daoism and development', in M. Clarke (ed.), *Handbook of research on religion and development*, Edward Elgar, Cheltenham, pp. 113–123.

Otto, R. 1950, *The idea of the holy*, trans. J.W. Harley, Oxford University Press, London.

Rabinow, P. 1984, *The Foucault reader*, Pantheon, New York.

Rist, G. 2014, *The history of development*, Zed Books, London.

Rae, L. & Clarke, M. 2013, 'Australian development FBOs and NGOs', in M. Clarke, (ed.), *Handbook of research on religion and development*, Edward Elgar, London, pp. 570–584.

Rees, J. 2011, *Religion in international politics and development: The World Bank and faith institutions*, Edward Elgar, Cheltenham.

Rostow, W. 1960, *The stages of economic growth*, Cambridge University Press, Cambridge.

Segal, E. 2009, *Introducing Judaism*, Routledge, London.

Seiple, R. & Hoover, D. (eds.) 2004, *Religion and security: The new nexus in international relations*, Rowman and Littlefield, Lanham.

Sen, A. 1999, *Development as freedom*, Oxford University Press, New York.

Sihlongonyane, M.F. 2003, 'The rhetoric of the community in project management: The case of Mohlakeng township', *Development in Practice*, vol. 11, no. 1, pp. 34–44.

Soja, Ew 1989, *Postmodern geographies: The reassertion of space in critical social theory*, Verso, London.

Soja, Ew 1996, *Thirdspace: Journeys to Los Angeles and other real and imagined places*, Blackwell, Oxford.

Stiglitz, J.E. 1999, 'The role of participation in development', *Development Outreach*, Summer 1999 1999, World Bank, Washington, pp. 1–4.

ter Haar, G. (ed.) 2011, *Religion and development: Ways of transforming the world*, Hurst Publications, London.

Tomalin, E., Starkey, C. & Halafoff, A. 2015 'Cyber sisters: Buddhist women's online activism and practice', in D. Enstedt, G. Larrson & E. Pace (eds.), *Religion and internet*, Annual Review of the Sociology of Religion Series vol. 6, Brill, Leiden and Boston, pp. 11–33.

Truman, H. 1949, *Inaugural address*, viewed 8 October 2015, https://www.trumanlibrary.org/whistlestop/50yr_archive/inagural20jan1949.htm.

United Nations Developemen Programme (UNDP) (1990), *Human development report*, UNDP, New York.

Urry, J. 1985, 'Social relations, space and time,' in D. Gregory and J. Urry (eds.), *Social relations and spatial structures*, St. Martin's Press, New York, pp. 21–48.

van der Leeuw, G. (1938) *Religion in essence and manifestation*, trans. J.E. lbrner, Princeton University Press, Princeton, original work published in German 1933.

Watson, B. & Clarke, M. 2014, *Child sponsorship: Exploring pathways to a brighter future*, Palgrave MacMillan, London.

Williams, A.M. 2007, 'Introduction: The continuing maturation of the therapeutic landscape concept', in A.M. Williams (ed.), *Therapeutic Landscapes*, Ashgate, Aldershot, pp. 1–12.

2 Vanuatu and Christian Churches

Introduction

Vanuatu is a Pacific island state consisting of an archipelago of more than 80 islands. The majority of Vanuatu's 270,000 population live on five main islands: Espiritu Santo, Malakula, Efate, Pentecost, and Tanna. While the main urban centre of Efate (on the island of Efate) is home to around 60,000 people, the rest of the population live in rural areas relying primarily on subsistence agriculture and small-scale cash-cropping. With a small population Vanuatu faces many development constraints common to similar island states, including social and political challenges brought about by a small and geographically dispersed population, difficult geography, reliance on volatile foreign aid, poor terms of trade, and limited comparative advantage (Feeny 2014, Leach et al. 2013a). Clarke et al. (2014) have found that poverty in Vanuatu (as measured by the Multidimensional Poverty Index)[1] is around 16 per cent, though this increases to one-quarter of households in the main urban centre of Port Vila on the island of Efate. Of further concern is that 42 per cent of Vanuatu households face some deprivation within one or more areas of health, education, standard of living or access to various support services meaning that a very significant proportion of the population that do not currently live in poverty are very vulnerable to falling into such poverty. Community development is therefore key to improving wellbeing across Vanuatu.

As noted above, Vanuatu is highly reliant on foreign aid, but there are substantial community development activities being undertaken by local organisations that do have significant impact, with local Christian Churches[2] being most prominent amongst them (see Clarke 2013). Given the history of Vanuatu, this prominence of Christian Churches in the social and economic development of Vanuatu is not surprising. As with many other Pacific nations, there has been a long history of Christian missions leading to strong locally led Churches providing leadership and practical educational and social services across the country. Indeed, initial mission activity[3] has resulted in more than 95 per cent of Ni-Vanuatu presently self-identifying as Christian (Vanuatu NSO 2009).[4] Whilst the introduction of Christian beliefs was problematic in some regards and did directly impact existing spiritual beliefs (Hilliard 1978), there is little doubt of the central role the Christian Churches play within Vanuatu today. From the first mission visit by the London Missionary Society in 1839 followed by more regular and then permanent missions of Anglicans and Presbyterians in 1849, the Christian Churches focused on provision of education and health services (Hilliard 1978). This community-focus of the Christian Churches further continued with the arrival of new missions from other Christian denominations (the French-speaking Catholic missionaries in 1887, Churches of Christ in 1901, Seventh Day Adventists in 1912, Apostolic Church in 1946 and so on) and occurred in an environment of neglect by the two colonial powers of Britain and France.[5]

Perhaps different to the experiences in other parts of the world, these early Christian missionaries quickly allowed local Ni-Vanuatu to assume leadership within the Church structures – from local ordained ministers to senior bureaucrats running national Church-run education and health services (Regenvanu 2004). This localisation of the Christian Churches has shaped the social and political development of Vanuatu and was essential, for example, in agitating for and then achieving independence in 1980 (Clarke 2015). Indeed, it was the Presbyterian General Synod that first called for independence almost a decade before it was achieved, becoming the first organisation to make such a public statement. Church leaders then continued to discuss and organise the wider Vanuatu population for independence. During this time, it was illegal for people to meet in public places to discuss such political issues, so in order to avoid the scrutiny of the political authorities, they often chose to meet in local churches. This was appropriate as the primary figures in the independence movements were Church leaders – predominantly ordained Church leaders (Regenvanu 2004). Thus meeting in these buildings avoided the scrutiny of authorities.[6]

Following on from this history, the role of the Christian Churches in undertaking community development in Vanuatu continues today. Core to the ability of the Christian Churches in undertaking on-going development of Vanuatu is the central role that they have in Vanuatu society. Not only is Christianity the dominant religious belief professed by Ni-Vanuatu, the long history of the Christian Churches providing social and education services and providing leadership for local and national communities has meant that daily life is interwoven with their faith, with Christianity being the centre (literally) of community life. In every community, there is a church more often than not located in a prominent position. Whether this is in urban areas or in rural villages, the church (or churches) is physically located so it is accessible to everyone. Given the patriarchal nature of Melanesian society (Eriksen 2008), the traditional spaces for decision-making largely exclude women. The *nakamal*, which is the *kastom* house for village or community meetings (generally restricted to men) is where (male) community leaders gather to discuss issues and make decisions concerning their communities. Alongside this traditional place though sits the church and its associated buildings. Unlike the nakamal, the church is open to both men and women. As a result, churches and other associated church buildings have become important spaces for both men and women to come together to both worship but also to continue to undertake community development activities to enhance the wellbeing of their communities and nation. It is actually quite common in the larger communities for there to be a number of buildings within the grounds of the church. These buildings may include a community hall, meeting spaces for various church groups, housing for the local pastor, school, health clinic, and so forth. These buildings may have multiple uses but all are located within the church grounds and are considered by community members as part of the 'the church'. In smaller communities, the church itself will often be used for the multiple purposes stated above.

This chapter will consider two examples where churches and church buildings have been the primary space for community development activities within Vanuatu. The first case study will be of the Presbyterian Women's Missionary Union (PWMU) and the second will be the use of churches as evacuation sites and distribution centres during and following Cyclone Pam in early 2015. Six PWMU participants were interviewed for this case study and commented on the PWMU's activities,[7] in particular the Let's Read programme and also the role of church spaces in disaster relief efforts during and after Cyclone Pam. Both these examples demonstrate the fluid movement between sacred place to development space in Christian Churches in Vanuatu and the coalescence of space and place in these circumstances.

Presbyterian Women's Missionary Union

The Presbyterian Church is the largest denomination in Vanuatu. With more than a quarter of the population professing religious adherence to the Presbyterian creed, it has more than 65,000 members (almost twice the number of the second largest denomination; Anglicanism). Of the six provinces,[8] members of the Presbyterian Church are the largest in Sanma (including the large island of Santo), Malampa (including the large island of Malekula), Shefa (including the most populous of all Vanuatu islands Efate), and Tafea (including the large island of Tanna). Given the historical missionary patterns with some islands being 'allocated' to certain missionary denominations, it is not surprising that there is almost no Presbyterian presence in Torba or Penama provinces (where the earliest of Christian missionaries – the Anglicans – were first active in Vanuatu) (Hilliard 1978).

The PWMU is part of the Presbyterian Church but is organised and structured as a separate entity. In this regard, it manages its finances and employs a General Secretary and Treasurer to oversee and manage the operations of the PWMU across Vanuatu. Every Presbyterian church has a PWMU associated with it, with every congregation electing a President, Vice President, Secretary and Treasurer. Each year, representatives from these congregations hold an annual conference where these same positions are elected for the national committee. Not all female members of the Presbyterian Church are members or active with the PWMU. Women may be too busy with family responsibilities, have work commitments, the local meeting times may be inconvenient, or they may not have the support of their husband in joining (though this is less of a issue than in the past). In urban areas, there are fewer younger women who are members compared to rural areas, but in urban areas younger women tend to join when they become mothers. In 2013, there were 7,645 registered members of the PWMU across Vanuatu, this included 478 members (within six sessions) in Ambrym Presbytery, 859 members (within 14 sessions) in Central Island Presbytery, 1,990 members (within six sessions) in Efate Presbytery, 1,560 members (within 15 sessions) in Santo Presbytery, 2,014 members (within 21 sessions) in Malekula Presbytery and 744 members (within 14 sessions) in South Island Presbytery (Participant A 2015).

Local PWMU chapters meet weekly. Depending on the buildings available to the local congregation, this will be either within the church itself or within the church hall (which is always co-located to the church and sits within the church compound). As Participant A (2015) explained, depending on the preference of the PWMU, the women 'go into the church for the meeting and use it as a meeting place'. The Vanuatu headquarters of the PWMU is located within the grounds of the Paton Memorial Church.

The Paton Memorial Church is the largest Presbyterian church in Vanuatu. It sits on the site of the first substantial church built by Presbyterian missions at the turn of the twentieth century. Following the significant damage to that church during a cyclone, the Paton Memorial Church was built and opened in 1959. It sits opposite Independence Park – while Vanuatu was under colonial control this public space was known as British Paddock as it sat adjacent to the British High Commission. It is a large A-frame building reminiscent of traditional Vanuatu buildings. The apex of the building is about 12 metres high with the roof sloping sharply to the ground. Its interior is sparsely decorated with a small altar and pulpit. The floor is unadorned concrete and the congregation sits on wooden pews with an aisle down the centre. When additional seats are required, individual metal chairs are placed alongside the wooden pews. While the church runs north-south, large doors on either side of the church (facing east-west) can be opened to allow the sea-breeze flow through the building providing natural air-conditioning. The church can hold 300 people. When larger church celebrations are held, the congregation overflows to the grassed lawns that surround three sides of the church. Within the same compound sit the Presbyterian Church offices, including the office of the Presbyterian Missionary Women's Union. These offices also house an eye clinic, the education office, and other outreach services associated with the Presbyterian Church.

The PWMU was formed in 1945 by two Australian missionaries, Miss Amy Skinner and Miss Kath Ritchie (Massam 2014). Both women were providing maternal and child health care as nurses on the small island of Ifira (which sits opposite the main town of Vila). In the course of their medical work, both Skinner and Ritchie became keenly aware of the wider needs of these mothers and their children and families. Understanding the constraints on women in traditional Vanuatu communities, Skinner and Ritchie set about to establish a fellowship programme that local women would be allowed to attend. At this time, Ni-Vanuatu women enjoyed limited freedom. Participant A (2015) stated that culturally their 'role was to be at home, tending gardens, and being in the kitchen. Women did not have freedom to decide where to go and whom to visit and had limited rights in front of men'. Understanding this, Skinner and Ritchie established the PWMU to initially provide fellowship opportunities for women and 'husbands agreed to let them join this fellowship' (Participant A 2015).

Soon the focus of these gatherings extended beyond traditional fellowship and Skinner and Ritchie began including activities that focused on the lived experiences of these women. These activities included weaving, cooking and housework. These practical skills also included English language training. Prayer and maternal and child health care remained cornerstones of the PWMU fellowship activities. As a result though, households of women who attended had less illness and sickness because of improved hygiene and more nutritional cooking. Consequently, increasing numbers of husbands were soon encouraging their wives to participate as material improvements in households were becoming increasingly evident as a result (Participant A 2015).

It did not take very long for the PWMU to move from the island of Ifra to the main island of Efate under the leadership of local Ni-Vanuatu women. From Ifira, the PWMU established itself in the local Presbyterian churches in the urban centres, and then spread to more rural churches around Efate; gradually becoming established in all islands of Vanuatu where there were Presbyterian congregations. As the PWMU expanded across Vanuatu, its aim remained steadfast to its origins: to spread the good news of the Bible through fellowship, and providing practical help to women at the local level by offering opportunities to learn new skills and enhance knowledge around issues that were grounded in the day to day realities of these women's lives (Participant B 2015).

The PWMU has four guiding principles that today drive its work. These principles are known as the 4Ss: spirituality, service, social, study. These four Ss are inspired by Scriptural verses (Participant B 2015). The focus on the whole person reflects Luke 2: 52, 'Jesus grew both in body and in wisdom, gaining favor with God and people'.

At its core, the PWMU remains an organisation interested in the spiritual welfare of its members and the wider community. As Participant B (2015) noted, Matthew 28: 19–20 extols Christians to '[g]o, then, to all peoples everywhere and make them my disciples: baptise them in the name of the Father, the Son, and the Holy Spirit and teach them to obey everything I have commanded you'. PWMU activities always start and end in prayer and bible studies and other education programmes highlight the centrality of Christian teaching in improving people's lives.

According to Participant C (2015), members of the PWMU also take seriously the concept of service, inspired by Acts 16: 13–15.

> On the Sabbath we went out of the city to the riverside, where we thought there would be a place where Jews gathered for prayer. We sat down and talked to the women who gathered there. One of those who heard us was Lydia from Thyatira, who was a dealer in purple cloth. She was a woman

> who worshiped God, and the Lord opened her mind to pay attention to what Paul was saying. After she and the people of her house had been baptised, she invited us, 'Come and stay in my house if you have decided that I am a true believer in the Lord.' And she persuaded us to go.

Visits to new mothers, widows, women with large families or suffering domestic violence are regular and important activities undertaken by PWMU members. Caring for their neighbours and community members can be practically orientated through the tending of gardens for these women struggling with other pressures or simply by home visits to overcome loneliness or provide moral support during times of loss or violence. The PWMU also provides social opportunities for its members. From its inception when local women had limited opportunity to mix outside of immediate families and communities, the PWMU provides a 'sanctioned' opportunity for women to come together in social settings. These social events may include visits to cultural sites or provide opportunities for fundraising activities to support some of their other programmes (Participant A 2015).

While training to improve skills that are household-focused, such as sewing, cooking, hygiene and sanitation remain common in PWMU-organised study activities, incursions and excursions that focus on more community-wide issues such as the environment, climate change, agriculture and health are also auspiced by the PWMU. According to Participant B (2015), following the exhortation to look at the whole in 1 Corinthians 12: 12–20, this wide focus is based on the knowledge that:

> Christ is like a single body, which has many parts; it is still one body, even though it is made up of different parts. In the same way, all of us, whether Jews or Gentiles, whether slaves or free, have been baptised into the one body by the same Spirit, and we have all been given the one Spirit to drink. For the body itself is not made up of only one part, but of many parts. If the foot were to say, 'Because I am not a hand, I don't belong to the body,' that would not keep it from being a part of the body. And if the ear were to say, 'Because I am not an eye, I don't belong to the body,' that would not keep it from being a part of the body. If the whole body were just an eye, how could it hear? And if it were only an ear, how could it smell? As it is, however, God put every different part in the body just as he wanted it to be. There would not be a body if it were all only one parts. As it is, there are many parts but one body.

Often in partnership with government or non-government organisations, these study opportunities provide members of the PWMU to engage in issues that affect the whole of society.

It is the last of the 4Ss that is most closely linked to the larger Presbyterian Church. The PWMU has a five-year plan that is drawn from the five-year plan of the General Synod. The five-year plan is discussed at the annual PWMU conference with yearly programmes established, which are then localised at the congregational level. Within the structure of the Vanuatu Presbyterian Church therefore, there exists a national plan, Presbytery level plans, Sessional level plans, Congregational level plans and finally church level plans. All of these plans support and link to each other. The current five-year plan (PWMU 2014) for 2014 to 2018 lists seven primary foci:

- Preaching
- Let's Read programme
- Gender and Leadership
- Personal Viability (livelihoods training)
- Health and Well-being
- Theology Training
- Health Worker

Within these areas, a number of activities are undertaken, including supporting microfinance schemes, training in bookkeeping, sewing, tourism and catering. PWMU members also undertake a wide range of visitations as part of their commitment to their communities. Those that they regularly visit include widows and widowers, the sick, recently born babies and their mothers, those in hospital, prisoners (and their families), wives of Pastors, those with disabilities, recently bereaved, elderly people without spouses or families, overseas students and single mothers (PWMU 2014).

Let's Read

With the financial support of Uniting Care (faith-based organisation located in Australia), the PWMU has instigated a Let's Read[9] programme (Pikinni Play Group) for babies aged five months to three years across five sites in and around Port Vila. These groups meet weekly with an early-childhood teacher employed across the five locations to coordinate and run the groups. While some of these centres do take place in church halls, there are a number that are located within churches themselves.

Partway up a hill on the peri-urban outskirts of Port Vila, the Pakarua Presbyterian Church sits nestled within thick green vegetation. The church is a squat solid building made largely of concrete. Attached alongside this church proper is a small annex used for Sunday School lessons but on Tuesday morning it becomes the location for the local Let's Read playgroup. The annex is quite a basic building. It has a corrugated iron roof, concrete floors and painted concrete walls. It is about 10 metres square with some wooden furniture and bookshelves around the edges. Children and their mothers sit on mats on the floor to play their games and there is a string between roughly hewn posts that hold drying paintings completed by the children. This is a relatively new group but its numbers are expanding quickly through word of mouth. The 30 children who regularly attend this playgroup were actually about to move to the larger church hall, which sits adjacent to this building, giving the children and their mothers (and grandmothers) more room to play.

This Let's Read programme is unique within Vanuatu. While some private crèches do exist, there is no government subsidised day care or other support for playgroups. Children's first experiences of any organised educational activities are therefore when they arrive at school aged five or six. The Let's Read playgroup has two primary purposes. The first is to provide age-appropriate education opportunities to children aged under five, and the second is to provide a support network for mothers of these children (Participant E 2015).

Within Vanuatu, it is not usual for children to have access to a range of toys. At this programme run in the Sunday School hall annexed to the church, there are a range of toys and games the young children freely play with. These include: blocks, Lego, paint, plasticine, sand games, puzzles, chalk, coloured marker pens and pencils, toy cars, dolls, and age-appropriate books. Parents are encouraged to borrow books to read to their children between weekly classes.

The two-hour sessions are facilitated by a trained early childhood teacher. While much of the two hours is free play, there are some structured activities built into the programme. This includes the reading of stories, repetitive singing of nursery songs, and a communal morning tea (parents bring some healthy snacks to share across the children). While the programme is run in Bislama (the primary language within Vanuatu) the structured activities are often in English to provide some exposure to the language of tuition in the majority of Vanuatu schools.[10] These activities include singing nursery rhymes, reading stories and playing games.

A nurturing network for mothers is also purposely developed within this Let's Read programme. Issues of childhood health, nutrition and hygiene are discussed in informal ways. Indeed, 'mothers enjoy being there. Otherwise they would most likely be home on their own and often bored' (Participant D 2015). While these playgroups are auspiced through the PWMU, each group is largely self-managed with their own Treasurer and organising committee. So while the PWMU provide the teacher, the mothers themselves organise themselves around fundraising and other required duties (Participant E 2015).

While not all participants are members of the Presbyterian Church, neither the hosting of this activity within the Presbyterian Church compound, nor its facilitation by the PWMU is an issue or point of contention for members. Church buildings are widely considered community facilities and so they are often used in Vanuatu for many non-denominational specific events. As Participant B (2015) described: 'They belong to the community. It is where the community is.' In a context where there is a lack of community facilities,[11] church buildings are presumed to be these community spaces.[12] Not only are these buildings located centrally within communities (both within urban, peri-urban and rural locations) they are generally provided for use without charge – including to government agencies.

This does not suggest that Pastors responsible for churches in Vanuatu do not have any control over their facilities. They do and permission must be received to run activities in their buildings. One of the advantages of the PWMU though, is that as it is formally part of the Presbyterian Church such relationships with local Pastors are generally very strong and support is given to allow the use of church buildings in support of PWMU activities (Participant C 2015).

Churches as sanctuary

Churches have long provided a sanctuary to those in need or those seeking to escape prosecution. Indeed, the term 'sanctuary' is taken from the name of the sanctified area around the altar of a church. On 13 March 2015 the second most intense tropical cyclone to ever affect the South Pacific (and the worst to affect Vanuatu) wrecked havoc across the country. Thousands of Ni-Vanuatu sought sanctuary in their local churches and church buildings. In the days following this devastating cyclone, these same buildings were central to the immediate relief efforts in terms of distribution sites and locales for on-going shelter for those whose houses were destroyed (Participant A 2015).

Vanuatu is one of the most disaster prone countries in the world (Welle and Birkmann 2015). Given its geographical location, Vanuatu is subject to earthquakes, cyclones, drought, floods, sea surge, climate change, and volcanoes. This risk is further exacerbated by the lack of coping and adaptive capacities within the country – largely as a result of lack of resources. While Vanuatu averages two to three tropical cyclones per year, it has recorded up to nine in twelve months (PCCSP 2013). As a result, the government and civil society – including the Churches – now give much greater attention to disaster preparedness. While Cyclone Pam hit Vanuatu on 13 March, its increasing intensity and development and likely path was known for much of the preceding week. During this time, as Cyclone Pam continued to deepen and strengthen, plans were put in place across Vanuatu for its impact and for the required response. Governments, NGOs and other constituents of civil society (including the Christian Churches) urged people to find shelter and prepare for the worst.[13] Such advice was appropriate given the severity of the cyclone with sustained winds of 250 kilometres per hour being recorded at the height of its strength. The importance of this advice is further evidenced when considering the construction materials of traditional housing. Outside of the main urban centres, traditional materials are still widely used in the construction of houses and other buildings. Such building materials include roughly hewn timber poles, woven bamboo matting for walls and thatched roofs. These materials are sometimes used in conjunction with concrete blocks and cast iron roof sheets. While entirely appropriate to the climate and availability of resources, these traditionally built houses do lack a certain structural integrity in the face of cyclonic winds. However, that is also an advantage, for should the building collapse there is limited risk of physical trauma from being caught underneath it. Indeed, it was most likely a combination of the forewarning for people to seek shelter in more strongly constructed buildings and the use of traditional housing materials that resulted in there being only approximately 20 reported deaths as a result of Cyclone Pam.

Having heeded the advice given as to the severity of Cyclone Pam, many people in urban and rural centres did relocate to buildings that were built of stronger materials for protection. Given the centrality of Christianity to the culture of Vanuatu, it is not surprising therefore that churches and church-buildings accounted for many of these structures. Indeed, in both urban and rural communities, the church was often the most substantial building in the area. For this reason, people were advised to seek shelter in them. While churches and church buildings differ from denomination to denomination, and community to community, they are commonly permanent structures built with quality materials and with attention to detail. As buildings whose primary purpose is worship, these buildings are physical expressions of the communities' faith and commitment to their religion. Churches across Vanuatu (particularly in urban areas) were often constructed with the financial support of partner churches in Australia or New Zealand (and occasionally the United States[14]) whose members were in some instances involved in the planning and construction itself. In the large urban centres the larger churches are often four or five decades old and have withstood annual cyclones (though none greater than Cyclone Pam).

In more rural locations, local communities have fund-raised amongst themselves to build their church and expended greater efforts and resources on these buildings then their own homes or schools as an expression of their religious faith. While there is no 'typical' Vanuatu style of church – with some incorporating certain Melanesia styles of A-frame roofs to or near the ground (such as the Paton Memorial Church described above), but others being squat square buildings – they are built with permanence in mind. Thus, many will have concrete floors, corrugated iron roofs, concrete brick walls, and steel beams for support. According to the Pastor Shem Tema, Chair of the Vanuatu Christian Council, 'church buildings are often the strongest buildings in communities. From our Ni-Vanuatu construction advisors' observations of villages across Vanuatu, almost every single village has a strong church, but, not every village has a strong school or village' (*Daily Post* 2015, p. 5). It was to these buildings that many thousands of Ni-Vanuatu sought refuge and sanctuary on the advice of the government, NGOs and civil society – as Cyclone Pam approached and then directly impacted Vanuatu (Participant F 2015).

Late on 13 March and throughout the night, winds roared across Vanuatu, stripping trees of their foliage, tearing down houses, strewing gardens with household belongings (clothes, furniture and toys), and ripping down power lines. All that night, rain flooded into buildings, collapsing roofs, ruining gardens and crops, and surging into low-lying areas. For those that had sought sanctuary in church buildings, the hours spent in darkness listening to deafening winds was only made worse when they ventured out the following morning to survey the damage and be faced with scenes of significant devastation with whole communities destroyed. Across the entire country, it was estimated that around two-thirds of the population was impacted by this storm, including more than

80,000 children (UNICEF 2015). In the urban centres, telecommunications, electricity, water, sewerage, and food markets were all disrupted for the first few days following the cyclone. While in some outlying areas, it took up to two weeks for some communities to receive assistance (United Nations 2015).

During and immediately following Cyclone Pam, the churches played an important role beyond that as a place of sanctuary during the height of the cyclone. Once the cyclone had passed, these same churches become focal points for providing both short-term shelter to those (many) people whose houses were destroyed, but also as places of distribution as part of the relief response. This role was formally recognised by the government of Vanuatu, which included the Christian Churches into the formal disaster response efforts, involving assisting with the assessment of damage following the cyclone on outer islands and in regional communities (VCC and Act for Peace 2015). In this instance the government recognised the value of the Churches existing and their extensive local networks.

Indeed, as Cyclone Pam was approaching Vanuatu and gaining in strength, the Vanuatu government approached the VCC to have churches used as part of the evacuation network (VCC and Act for Peace 2015). More than 50 churches were officially utilised as evacuation centres in the days and weeks following the cyclone (*Daily Post* 2015). So on Saturday afternoon people voluntarily or with assistance from church members and leaders began to congregate within these churches as the cyclone approached. As Participant A (2015) recounted: 'People felt to go inside churches they would be safe, as they always felt safe in church.' At different locations upwards of 150 to 200 people sought shelter in these various churches. That the total number of deaths as a result of the cyclone was quite low, can be in part explained by the fact that so many people sought shelter in these 'permanent' buildings.

Even though people knew ahead of time that Cyclone Pam was going to be the most severe cyclone experienced in living memory, the devastation was still shocking. Buildings that were considered strong were destroyed, new houses had roofs blown away, and the driving rain flooded houses, destroying furniture, bedding, clothes, and books. The cleanup began immediately on the day following the cyclone. With a sunny morning, people began to collect up their remaining possessions and lay them out to dry. However, further rains came later that afternoon and put these plans to an end. Participant B (2015) surmised: 'The destroyed houses just represented destroyed lives.' Imported food quickly ran out and much garden food was destroyed. What did make it to market in the days that followed was quickly purchased despite high prices.[15]

The damage was not simply contained to the infrastructure and agriculture. The power of the cyclone and the damage it wrought also resulted in an emotional toll on many inhabitants across Vanuatu. In recognition of this, the Presbyterian Church quickly brought together its pastors, elders, and PWMU leaders to attend a two-day workshop. Held in the Paton Memorial Church hall in Port Vila, this two-day event focused on the emotional needs that the church would now have to address in addition to the more obvious infrastructural reconstruction. This emotional reconstruction focused on six steps of recovery:

- Dealing with the shock of the event
- Dealing with the sense of loss of control
- Dealing with activities to prevent future losses
- Dealing with reality of current losses
- Planning actions to respond
- Establishing hope in order to move forward (Participant A 2015)

The Presbyterian Church believed it important that this response to Cyclone Pam be a national response and so passed its resources through to the national government for them to co-ordinate the distribution response across the nation. Such a response was based on Scriptural teaching of sharing resources inspired by Acts 4: 32–35.

> All the believers were one in heart and mind. No one claimed that any of their possessions was their own, but they shared everything they had. With great power the apostles continued to testify to the resurrection of the Lord Jesus. And God's grace was so powerfully at work in them all that there were no needy persons among them. For from time to time those who owned land or houses sold them, brought the money from the sales and put it at the apostles' feet, and it was distributed to anyone who had need...

However, the government was also very cognisant of the existing and extensive church networks and was able to use these for the distribution of resources; including the use of churches as distribution and storage centres. These networks provided access to even the most rural and remote communities.

Following the cyclone, these churches continued to play an important role in the immediate response. People used them for shelter as much of the population suffered damage to their own homes, but they were also importantly utilised as distribution points for dissemination of supplies. Whilst some churches were damaged during the cyclone, they resumed their important role as natural community hubs in the days immediately following the cyclone. As Participant F (2015) explained, not only were these often the first buildings to be cleaned and repaired, they were where people naturally congregated for support and assistance.

The value of the churches as community centres was recognised by NGOs who were able to leverage this community asset in their response planning. Across Vanuatu, organisations such as Save the Children were able to utilise these buildings and personnel in their formal distribution networks. Not only were these churches and church buildings safe and secure locations for the storage of relief supplies, the local church leaders were often very well placed to provide logistical information as to the community, including information as to whom had been affected, and the extent of damage. Not needing to establish distribution sites made the provision of supplies to affected families and communities quicker but also more efficient (Participant B 2015).

As noted above, there is very strong likelihood that further natural disasters will affect Vanuatu. Prior to Cyclone Pam, the government and civil society were undertaking regular disaster preparedness planning. Such activities will continue in its aftermath. The value and importance of the churches in Vanuatu has been both recognised and evidenced but at the same time resisted. Presently, the inclusion of churches in official rebuilding programmes is unresolved. Thus, despite the role played by churches and Church networks during and after Cyclone Pam, the government of Vanuatu has excluded the building or repairing of churches within the official recovery planning. This decision has been met with strong resistance by the Vanuatu Christian Council (VCC) who argue that:

> The church buildings are used for a variety of community activities including women's group meetings, space to prepare materials for sale, youth meetings and so forth. They are the hub of the community, supporting spiritual, social and counseling needs.
>
> Church and religion are an integral part of community life in Vanuatu, to try to make a distinction between 'churches' and 'a community' is to create an artificial separation which does not reflect the reality of Vanuatu life.
>
> Recovery is more than physical recovery. It is also about emotional recovery. Churches provide important services in recovery of all kinds.
>
> (Pastor Shem Tema, Chair of VCC, *Daily Post* 2015, p. 5)

The final determination is still to be made and as the recovery phase will continue for up to five years, it is not possible to say with any finality whether these church buildings will be included or excluded over the course of this period. What is clear though is that these sacred buildings have been a core component of the response to the worst cyclone experienced in Vanuatu in living memory and played very positive roles in protecting Ni-Vanuatu across the country. In this instance, they have most certainly been places of sanctuary.

Conclusion

Since the earliest days of missionary activity in Vanuatu – now approaching 200 years – to the present, the Christian Churches have played a prominent role in the social and political development of Vanuatu. With a focus on the provision of health and educational social services and providing local leadership opportunities, the Christian Churches have been central to how Vanuatu as a nation currently exists. Many of the activities undertaken to this end by the Christian Churches have occurred within church places of worship or associate church buildings. Without this physical location in which to plan, implement and evaluate these multiple activities, it is unlikely that these development interventions would have occurred or been as successful.

Christian churches in Vanuatu are open to both men and women. Unlike traditional decision-making locations (the nakamal), women and men can attend and participate equally within these church buildings. The PWMU has played a significant role in improving the lives of Ni-Vanuatu for many decades. With their headquarters located within the church grounds of the Paton Memorial Presbyterian Church in Port Vila, its local members utilise churches and church buildings across Vanuatu to undertake a whole range of community development activities, including formal pre-school programmes to assist school readiness of young children. The stimulus for providing these development activities can be found in biblical texts that are shared and learned in these places of worship. The impetus to provide assistance and sanctuary to those in need come from the teachings of Christ found within the scriptures.

As a fundamental part of their personal and social identity, Christian churches are typically the most well-built structures in urban and rural communities. As an expression of their faith, high-quality building materials and on-going maintenance of these structures ensures that they are strong and long-lasting (in comparison with many traditional buildings). Given this quality of building, many churches across Vanuatu served as key sanctuaries during the devastating Cyclone Sam in early 2015. The government and NGOs (and the Churches themselves) encouraged people to use their local churches as shelter during the height of the cyclone. Following the cyclone and with their own homes destroyed, many people stayed in the churches and continued to shelter there. These churches also served as important distribution points in the recovery efforts in the following days and weeks.

As sacred places, these sanctified buildings across Vanuatu also play important roles as development spaces and facilitate and allow community development activities to occur. Within Vanuatu, churches and church buildings are simultaneously both places and spaces that have shaped Vanuatu's social and political development.

Notes

1 The global Multidimensional Poverty Index (MPI) was developed by the Oxford Poverty and Human Development Initiative (OPHI) (see Alkire and Foster 2011). The MPI measures a number of deprivations that a household experiences. More specifically, it calculates the percentage of households that experience overlapping deprivations in three dimensions: education; health; and living conditions.

2 Given the relatively ecumenical manner in which the different denominations – Anglican, Catholic, Presbyterian, Assemblies of God, Seventh Day Adventists, Apostolic, and Churches of Christ – in Vanuatu co-operate and advocate together under the auspices of the Vanuatu Christian Council, these main Christian denominations will be referred to collectively as the 'Christian Churches'. When the term 'church' – with a lower-case 'c' – is used, this will refer to buildings in which Christian worship takes place.

3 The first European contact with Vanuatu was the Spanish explorer Pedro Fernandez de Queiros in 1606. A temporary chapel was built, a Mass was held and two Ni-Vanuatu boys were baptised at this time (Beaglehole 1966).

4 The proportion of Ni-Vanuatu who are Christian is often cited as 83 per cent. This figure is drawn from the 2009 census. However it is based upon the misunderstanding that the 13 per cent nominating themselves as 'other' in the census are not Christian. Rather, the majority of respondents within this category are Christian, but not of the denominations listed on the census form: Presbyterian, Anglican, Catholic, SDA, Apostolic, Churches of Christ, Assemblies of God, Neil Thomas Ministries.

5 See Miles (1998) and Woodward (2014) for a description of the Condominium Government established between the British and French in 1907 and the dual occupancy of the then named New Hebrides prior to this.

6 However, there was some disquiet with non-Ni-Vanuatu missionaries who were concerned with the overtly political nature of this Independence movement. Some years after the General Synod Declaration on Independence and after one particular meeting in the Paton Presbyterian Church, the Independence leaders moved up the road to a restaurant in which they wrote the proposed Constitution. With thousands of people sitting outside the restaurant, the leaders on completion of the Constitution presented it to the massed throng with much celebration and excitement – at 3.00 a. m. in the morning (Regenvanu 2004).

7 The participants' anonymised comments are included in the chapter and cited as (Participant A-F 2015), as the interviews were conducted in 2015.

8 Provinces within Vanuatu are named after acronyms of the initial letters of the main constituent islands. Thus SHEFA is made up of the 'SHephard' and 'EFAte' islands.

9 The Let's Read programme is an established literacy programme developed in Australia – see www.letsread.com.au for further information about the programme. The PWMU received training and financial support through the Uniting Care South Gippsland branch in Victoria, Australia in 2011/12 to deliver this programme in Vanuatu.

10 Vanuatu has three official languages: Bislama, English and French. This is an outcome of the dual colonial rule of Vanuatu by the French and the British known as the Condominium.

11 Traditional community spaces were desegregated with the nakamal, the community space reserved for men and decision-making. Such spaces still exist across Vanuatu – often co-located with church buildings in the rural areas, but they are inappropriate for general community use.

12 Indeed, on the day of the site visit to the Let's Read programme at Pakarua Presbyterian Church, the adjacent church hall was being used by a government-funded maternal and child health nurse for her monthly community village meeting. Women and their babies from the local community were therefore being provided with immunisations and the service of weighing of their children in this facility within the grounds of the Presbyterian Church.

13 The large expatriate community primarily took shelter in their own homes or with international tourists in the large resorts.

14 Even within Vanuatu, churches of the Church of the Latter-Day Saints are typically built to US building regulations.

15 It was reported that the main hardware items required in the response (tarpaulins, iron sheeting, nails, etc.) were sold at cost as a sign of solidarity and goodwill by the largest hardware stores in the weeks following the cyclone. Some food stuffs, particularly rice, were also sold at cost by the largest supermarkets in the main town of Port Vila (Participant A 2015).

References

Alkire, S. & Foster, J. 2011, 'Counting and multidimensional poverty measurement', *Journal of Public Economics*, vol. 95, no. 7–8, pp. 476–487.

Beaglehole, J.C. 1966, *The exploration of the Pacific*, Stanford University Press, London.

Clarke, M. 2013, 'Good works and God's work: A case study of churches and community development in Vanuatu', *Asia Pacific Viewpoint*, vol. 54, no. 3, pp. 340–351.

Clarke, M. 2015, 'Christianity and the shaping of Vanuatu's social and political development', *Journal of the Academic Study of Religion*, vol. 28, no. 1, pp. 24–41.

Clarke, M., Feeny, S. & McDonald, L. 2014, 'Vulnerability to what? Multidimensional poverty in Melanesia', in S. Feeny (ed.), *Household vulnerability and resilience to economic shocks: Findings from Melanesia*, Ashgate, Farnham, pp. 83–106.

*Daily Post*2015, 'Include Churches in Gov't Recovery Management Framework: VCC', *Daily Post*, 3 June, p. 5.

Eriksen, A. 2008, *Gender, Christianity and Change in Vanuatu*, Routledge, London.

Eriksen, A. 2015, *Gender, Christianity and change in Vanuatu: An analysis of social movements in North Ambrym*, Ashgate, Aldershot.

Feeny, S. (ed.) 2014, *Household vulnerability and resilience to economic shocks: Findings from Melanesia*, Ashgate, Farnham.

Hilliard, D. 1978, *Gods gentlemen: A history of the Melanesian Mission 1849–1942*, University of Queensland Press, Brisbane.

Leach, M., Scambary, J., Clarke, M., Feeny, S. & Wallace, H. 2013, *Attitudes to national identity in Melanesia and Timor-Leste: A survey of future leaders in Papua New Guinea, Solomon Islands, Vanuatu, and Timor-Leste*, Peter Lang, Oxford.

Massam, K. 2014, 'Creating spaces between: Women and mission in Oceania', Keynote Address, Conference of the Association for Practical Theology in Oceania, Sydney, 27–0 November 2014.

Miles, W.F.S. 1998, *Bridging mental boundaries in a post-colonial microcosm: Identity and development in Vanuatu*, University of Hawaii Press, Honolulu.

Pacific Climate Change Science Program (PCCSP) 2013, *Current and future climate of Vanuatu*, Vanuatu Meteorology and Geo-Hazard Department, Port Vila.

Presbyterian Missionary Women's Union (PWMU) 2014, *PWMU Five Year Plan, 2014–2018*, PWMU, Port Vila.

Regenvanu, S. 2004, *Laef blong mi: From village to nation*, University of South Pacific Press, Suva.

United Nations Children's Fund (UNICEF) 2015, 'Cyclone Pam in Vanuatu', viewed 21 July 2015, www.unicef.org.nz/vanuatu.

United Nations 2015, 'Cyclone Pam: UN agency reports all 22 Vanuatu islands reached with relief supplies', viewed 21 July 2015, http://www.un.org/apps/news/story.asp?NewsID=50440#.Va2SquvIvuV.

Vanuatu Christian Council (VCC) and Act for Peace 2015, 'Vanuatu Christian evacuation centres need support', viewed on 23 July 2015, https://www.youtube.com/watch?v=8plVMQa0uEU.

Vanuatu National Statistical Office (NSO) 2009, *2009 National census of population and housing*, viewed 1 July 2012, http://www.vnso.gov.vu/images/stories/2009_Census_Summary_release_final.pdf.

Welle, T. and Birkmann, J. 2015, 'The WorldRiskIndex' in Bündnis Entwicklung Hilft, *WorldRiskReport 2015*, Bündnis Entwicklung Hilft,,Berlin.

Woodward, K. 2014, *A political memoir of the Anglo-French condominium of the New Hebrides*, ANU Press, Canberra.

3 Minhaj-ul-Quran International, charity and education[1]

Introduction

Minhaj-ul-Quran International's (MQI) headquarters are in central Lahore, in a district known as Model Town. A line of high white and green Islamic keel arches welcomes the visitor to this impressive complex. Beside it stands the Minara-tus-Salam building, with a golden crescent moon atop its large green and gold minaret. It is modelled on the shrine of Maulana Rum, the great Sufi teacher and poet Rumi, in Konya, Turkey. Both the inside and outside of this sacred place are inscribed with Islamic sacred texts, including verses from the Quran and the 99 names of Allah in blue and white Arabic calligraphy. The interior is also lined with beautiful blue, white, red and green patterned tiles, and the central gate and windows are made of solid carved wood. While the white walls of the Central Secretariat evoke both wisdom and purity, the green, gold, white and blue Minara-tus-Salam induces awe and wonder, yet has a warm inviting quality. The Minara-tus-Salam, also called Gosha-e-Durood, was opened by Shaykh-ul-Islam Dr Muhammad Tahir-ul-Qadri, MQI's founder and esteemed teacher, in 2005. Gosha-e-Durood is a sacred place where people can undertake a 'spiritual retreat' unique to MQI, 'reciting Salat [prayer] and Salam [peace] on the beloved Prophet Muhammad (SAW [peace be upon him])', honoring and respecting the Prophet, 24 hours a day, seven days a week, for 365 days a year. Around the corner is the Jamy Masjid Minhaj-ul-Quran Mosque, where the Minhaj Welfare Foundation (MWF) offices are located (GeD n.d.a, b; Qadri 2015).

One of the first major developments of MQI was the establishment of the Jamia Islamia Minhaj-ul-Quran, the College of Sharia and Islamic Sciences, in Lahore in 1986, within what later became the larger Minhaj University Lahore (MUL). The MUL is a fifteen minute drive from the MQI headquarters and provides a secular and Islamic University education for its students. MQI's Aghosh Orphanage, and Model School sites for boys and for girls, are housed on nearby premises next to the site of Itikaf City (Itikaf City n.d.a, b; Qadri 2015).

Fifty thousand worshippers come to Itikaf city annually to participate in an international spiritual gathering held in the last ten days of the Holy Month of

Ramadan each year. This is traditionally a time for seclusion/retreat, which is an optional Muslim practice that can be done alone or collectively. It is performed in many places including the Masjid al-Haram in Makkah and Masjid Nabavi in Madinah and is modelled on the collective Itikaf that the Holy Prophet (SAW) held in Masjid Nabavi, in which he delivered teachings and practical advice for spiritual development to his Sahabah (companions). During the retreat, the buildings within Itikaf City, and notably the Jamy Masjid Al-Minhaj, the Township Mosque and the Syed Tahir Alauddin Al-Qadri shrine adjacent to it, are draped in coloured lights to mark this festive occasion. The tens of thousands of people present fill all of the outdoor places as well as the buildings. Huge white marquee structures shade the participants, while large fans cool them down as they listen to teachings of Shaykh-ul-Islam and his sons, as well as other notable teachers. The Itikaf is described as a 'spiritual training camp' for seekers in which they learn about living in accordance with Islamic peacebuilding principles, including the importance of helping others (Itikaf City n.d. a, b; Qadri 2015; Mash'hadi 2015).

MQI's sacred places comprise its mosques and monuments, its educational and community centres, and shrines to saints within and nearby its centres, which have traditionally been sites for development activities.

Minhaj-ul-Quran International's origins

Shaykh-ul-Islam Dr Muhammad Tahir-ul-Qadri was born in Jhang, Pakistan on February 19, 1951. He was the son of a great Sufi teacher ash-Shaykh Dr Farida'd-Din al-Qadri and received both an Islamic and secular scientific education of the highest quality. He trained with his father, and other eminent Shuyukh in Pakistan and abroad, including ash-Shaykh Syed Tahir Alauddin Al-Qadri al-Gilani, a very pious and a great figure in Sufi Islam in recent times. Shaykh-ul-Islam obtained a formal classical Islamic education, from the age of twelve at the Madrasa al-'Ulum ash-Shar'iyya, in Madinah. He also received a First Class Honors Degree, an MA in Islamic Studies, and a Ph.D. in Islamic Law, all from the University of the Punjab where he worked as a lecturer and then Professor of Law. He soon became Pakistan's 'leading Islamic jurist and scholar and revivalist of the Islamic ideology' (Shaykh-ul-Islam 2011).

Shaykh-ul-Islam founded Minhaj-ul-Quran International in 1981, and established its international headquarters in Lahore, Pakistan. Currently, MQI is one of the world's largest non-government organisations with an international network spanning over 90 countries. Shaykh-ul-Islam was dissatisfied with the Islamic religious institutions and organisations in Pakistan at the time and formed MQI 'to promote and propagate true Islamic teachings and philosophy' (MQI n.d.b). Due to the rise of Islamist extremist movements who advocated the use of violence and terrorism at the turn of the twenty-first century, Shaykh-ul-Islam felt a strong need to respond and clarify the teachings of Islam and issued the historic *Fatwa on Terrorism* in 2010, directly refuting the ideology of the Taliban and al-Qaeda. He is a prolific writer and one of the most prominent Muslim Sufi leaders calling for an end to terror and advocating Islamic peacebuilding principles globally. Shaykh-ul-Islam has also been highly politically active in Pakistan. He founded the political party Pakistan Awami Tehreek (PAT) in 1989 and has initiated two anti-corruption and pro-democracy Long Marches in 2013 and 2014, the latter resulting in violent clashes with police and casualties among the PAT activists (MQI n.d.a; Qadri 2015).[2]

According to Shaykh-ul-Islam:

> The primary aim of the Minhaj-ul-Quran International is to bring about a comprehensive and multidimensional change in the society which at the same time ends the academic and ideological deadlock and revive, once again, the exterminated moral and spiritual values (of Islam), and also exalt the Muslim Umma to an admirable and respectful status among the comity of nations by a continuous struggle based on glorious foundation laid down by the Holy Prophet (blessings and peace be upon him) on the universal principles of Love, Peace and Knowledge.
>
> (MQI n.d.b)

MQI is focused on,

> working to promote peace, tolerance, interfaith harmony and education, tackle extremism and terrorism, engage with young Muslims for religious moderation, promote women's rights, development and empowerment, and provide social welfare and promotion of human rights.
>
> (MQI n.d.b)

MQI includes a number of institutions and organisations that further its mission and activities. These include: the Minhaj University Lahore, chartered by the Pakistan government, which provides both an Islamic and secular scientific education; the Minhaj Education Society (MES) which has currently established more than 625 schools and colleges in Pakistan; the Minhaj Welfare Foundation (MWF), a global humanitarian and social welfare organisation; the Minhaj-ul-Quran Ullama Council; the Minhaj-ul-Quran Women's League; the Minhaj Youth League; and the Muslim Christian Dialogue Forum (Shaykh-ul-Islam 2011, MQI n.d.b; Qadri 2015).

MQI's development activities are primarily centred on providing education, health care, social welfare and emergency relief to economically poorer people in and beyond Pakistan. The Minhaj Welfare Foundation (MWF) is the arm of MQI that coordinates these activities. Its head offices are in Lahore and London, with branches and projects in over 100 nations (MWF n.d.a).

MWF has a variety of programmes in South Asia, the Middle East, Africa and North America (MWF n.d.c). Their projects include the establishment of schools, colleges and libraries, hospitals, free medicine dispensaries and medical and eye surgery camps, free ambulance services, clean drinking water projects, financial assistance for marriages, and emergency relief after natural disasters such as tsunamis and earthquakes (MWF n.d.a).

The MWF website calls for and accepts donations for their current projects. Two initiatives that feature prominently on the website are the Agosh Orphan Care Home and the Qurbani programme. The Aghosh Orphanage in Lahore began to be built in 2008 and now provides a high-quality 'Hifz-e-Quran' [Islamic] and school education to 500 orphans, equipping them with skills to be of benefit to the wider community (MWF n.d.b). The Qurbani programme encourages people to perform charitable acts by donating funds that can purchase meat products to be distributed by MWF to those in need. Established in 1989, over 100,000 Qurbani packages have been distributed worldwide, assisting millions of people (MWF n.d.d).

Minhaj-ul-Quran International's education and welfare programmes

Dr Hussain Mohi-ud-Din Qadri,[3] the second son of Shaykh-ul-Islam, is an eminent Sufi teacher, President of MQI and Deputy Chairman of the Board of Governors of the Minhaj University Lahore (MUL), Chairman Minhaj Education Society (MES), and Chairman Aghosh Orphan Care Homes. He is an economist by profession and has a Ph.D. in economics from Victoria University, Melbourne, Australia. He completed his undergraduate studies with economics and political science as his majors at York University in Canada and his MBA from Sciences Po in Paris. Alongside his academic studies, he obtained an education in Islamic classic sciences from his father, and other well-respected teachers who were also students of Shaykh-ul-Islam (Qadri 2015).

Dr Qadri (2015) explained how his father first established MQI 'on the basis and ideology of human service and spirituality'. Given that his father is a Sufi master and that Pakistan is a majority Muslim society, MQI's foundation is the 'spiritual and Sufi philosophy of Islam, which is mainly based on helping each other'. Dr Qadri (2015) described how initially MQI focused on two main interconnected areas. First, education, through the establishment of schools that provide a regular secular and Islamic education, and second, 'improving and clarifying the actual image of Sufi Islam'.

Minhaj Education Society (MES) schools include subjects such as mathematics, social sciences, sciences, English and philosophy and also courses focused on 'character building' which are related to promoting 'the peaceful message of Islam and how a Muslim should be a peaceful human being… while interacting with others' (Qadri 2015). This distinguished MES schools from *madrassas* that concentrate mainly on providing a 'classical religious education'. Dr Qadri (2015) described how,

> a lot of time and efforts are put in and invested on the children to develop their character, to make them more humble, more peaceful in their lives,

> not fighting with each other, more tolerant in their personalities, and understanding, respecting to other religions and other communities.

Dr Qadri (2015) also stated that 150,000 students were enrolled in the MES network's schools, which employed over 10,000 teachers. 50 per cent of these students were receiving scholarships or 'at least, very reduced fee packages', which enabled them to attend the schools, with scholarships funded by donations. Most of these schools have been established in rural locations where previously there were limited opportunities for education. MQI's university is run on similar principles providing regular academic programmes in engineering or medicine for example, as well as Islamic sciences. Dr Qadri (2015) recounted how his father 'faced a lot of resistance from other religious corridors, political corridors' when developing MQI's education model, as previously secular and religious education were divided in Pakistan and it was an entirely new concept to deliver them together. Shaykh-ul-Islam has described MQI's programme as 'the revolution through education'.

According to Mr Dawood Mash'hadi[4] (2015), Managing Director of Minhaj Welfare Foundation (MWF), the vast majority of MWF's activities are focused on education as they believe that 'education is the key solution to 90 per cent of the problems which the poor, the needy people face all over the world'. He spoke of the importance of educating about basic concepts such as the need for clean water and cleanliness more generally, which are stressed in religious teachings.

> Cleanliness is part of the basic ethics of [every] religion. In Islam it's a famous saying of the Holy Prophet that half of your belief is cleanliness. So if you know how to keep your inner self clean, your outer self clean, and your surroundings [clean], you have done half of your religion of Islam... if you have clean water, clean clothes, clean home, clean surroundings, clean food to eat – you're automatically in an environment which saves you from diseases, which gives you a healthy life, long life.
>
> (Mash'hadi 2015)

Initially MWF set up projects to assist the poor by providing basic facilities, like shelter, food, wells, medical testing for blood pressure and blood sugar, and medicines and medical procedures such as cataract operations where needed. They also assisted with natural disaster relief, following earthquakes and floods, and human-made disaster relief in places affected by war and conflicts. Mr Mash'hadi (2015) believes volunteers are the 'driving force' of MWF as they do 90 per cent of its work. MWF is also completely funded by donations. MWF has established many programmes in Pakistan, but also internationally in countries such as Indonesia, Afghanistan, Kenya, and Somalia. Mr Mash'hadi (2015) noted that,

> [in] any country we work in we follow the principles, rules, and regulations of the local land... [to] make sure that it's all done legally, properly. That

> is the only way forward to keep it sustainable. And that's how we have been working for the past more than 25 years.

Mr Mash'hadi (2015) stated that when MWF provides assistance to local communities, they make sure that the community takes ownership of the projects in order to ensure their long-term success. For example, he explained how, when assisting a community to build a well, in a place where the future security of the well is frequently an issue, they always work in partnership with local teams of people.

> It's easy to build a water well, or install a water pump. But to make sure the ownership is taken by the local community is the key part that will keep it sustainable for the next five to ten years. And that's the key which Minhaj Welfare Foundation in a way specialises in engaging local community people, handing over the ownership to the local people. So that each… individual living in that community, in a way takes responsibility of saying 'yes I'm responsible, I will look after it, I'll clean it, I'll maintain it, and me and my kids, or me and my family will take the benefits of it'.
>
> (Mash'hadi 2015)

Mr Mash'hadi (2015) recounted that MQI's founder, Shaykh-ul-Islam, has been the main inspiration for MWF's activities and that he made sure that MWF assists not only Muslims but is focused on the whole of humanity, regardless of their religious affiliation. According to Mr Mash'hadi (2015), Shaykh-ul-Islam 'is an individual who knows how to bring and present Islam into the modern world', to assist Muslims and all of humanity and 'to ensure… that Islam is presented in every possible way correctly to the Muslims and to the Western world' especially given recent and current negative perceptions of Islam, and its association with violent extremism, that need to be corrected.

Sacred places and shrines

Another initiative that Shaykh-ul-Islam instigated, focused on character building through spiritual training, is the Itikaf City, a complex established beside the shrine of Shaykh Tahir Alauddin Al-Qadri, including a mosque with a large outdoor seating area, dormitories and shops, where people regularly spend the last ten days of the holy month of Ramadan on a spiritual retreat (Qadri 2015). Dr Qadri (2015) described the Itikaf as follows,

> there's thousands of people, sometimes it reaches up to 50,000 people, men and women. So they come there and they sit there for days and they fast together… They help each other. Then there are so many lessons and lectures, trainings going on during those ten days… spiritual trainings… [on] how to handle your arrogance… how to manage your anger, and… lectures on… how to behave, what kind of a life Islam desires… how you can become

> peaceful, how you can become more productive… at your workplace being a Sufi Muslim… how you can bridge your spiritual life and professional life together. So these kinds of trainings are going on… [and] a couple of holy activities as well… [such as] the remembrance of God, reciting the names of God… holy songs… so it's kind of a festival for ten days.

Dr Qadri (2015) added how the concept of Itikaf well predates MQI's founding.

> Itikaf is something which is there in the Holy Scriptures of Islam. So it is all related and has a history back to Moses when God Almighty invited him to Sinai for seclusion. First he was invited for ten days, then it became 20, 30 and then finally he sat there in seclusion for 40 days before he returned back to his people. So it all came from that concept that at least in 365 days of your life, once every year for ten days you go into the seclusion for the God… for his remembrance and also because there is another interesting concept in Islam… that one moment of deep thinking about what you have done right and what you have done wrong in your life… just a moment of that analysis is much more powerful and worthy of God's happiness than 70 years of straight non-stop worship. So this is ten days of realisation as well, spiritual realisation, inner realisation.

Dr Qadri (2015) described how people participating in Itikaf have reported that it has 'changed their personalities', giving them confidence, making them more honest and more balanced generally. With so many people present, and often in quite challenging physical circumstances, such as stormy weather, people learn a great deal about themselves and how to live harmoniously with one another. According to Dr Qadri (2015),

> what we have lost today, is the bond between humans and we have become too materialistic, we think about ourselves only and we hardly know what's happening next door, if somebody is sick or not we don't really care. We say that that's their business or that the government should take care of them… but [in the] early days all of the spiritualities, of the religions… they would say you should know if somebody is sleeping hungry next door or not… People used to care about each other… So this kind of an environment and activity, that helps people bring all those good moral tradition back to their lives. And once they sit there for ten days, when they go back everyone has new bonds and relations with each other… so it's kind of a new family they build up there.

While Dr Qadri (2015) said that 'Itikaf, in itself is not unique, everyone does it', usually individually or in much smaller groups of people, the emphasis that MQI's Itikaf places on community engagement and helping those in need is distinctive. The scale of the Itikaf City in Lahore also makes it the third largest Itikaf in the world, next to those held in Makkah and Madinah. An additional 'welfare based benefit to the community', which takes place during the ten days of Itikaf, is that over a million people are fed there. Dr Qadri (2015) explained,

> again from the Quran in Islamic preaching it comes that God loves those people, that if they have one loaf of bread and are hungry for three days, someone knocks at their door and they're hungry, rather than thinking I am myself hungry for three days... so they will take that loaf of bread and give it to that beggar.

Dr Qadri (2015) also described the Gosha-e-Durood practices that take place at the sacred monument site of Minara-tus-Salam as a 'mini Itikaf' that takes place continuously throughout the year in ten-day blocks. Each month, within 30 days, there are three sets of ten-day blocks in which 30 people participate. Ten people take the first eight-hour shift reciting specified prayers and verses from the Quran. For the remaining 16 hours of the day, they can attend lectures by Sufi scholars and also sleep. While they are doing so, another shift of people takes their place, praying in this 'very unique building'.

When asked why the Itikaf and its associated welfare activities takes place next to the Shaykh Tahir Alauddin Al-Qadri shrine, Dr Qadri (2015) replied, 'because the shrine is a holy and sacred place in Islam'. He explained that shrines are the gravesites of Muslim saints and that traditionally people visited them, and prayed to God at them, and also conducted welfare and educational activities beside them: 'We love shrines, we go to the shrine, we spend time there, we have such activities and festivals next to or in those shrines.' He stated that Muslims did not consider these saints to be God but rather pious humans 'who lived their life for God Almighty' so that 'God Almighty is happy with them'. Consequently, these saints are 'great role models' for ordinary people to aspire to. Given their inspirational lives and charitable deeds, 'wherever even they are sleeping or their bodies are, so that place is a blessed place'.

Dr Qadri (2015) further explained how people do not pray to the shrines themselves or to the saints but to Allah.

> We go there, we pray to God Almighty by saying that 'oh God we are sitting or standing here in this place where your blessed man is lying or sleeping... we pray to you, that you can help us fulfil our desire'... So it is said if you pray while standing in those blessed places, where the God chosen ones are sleeping, it is more likely that God will listen to you.

Dr Qadri (2015) elaborated,

> bringing them and making them sit next to such sacred places... they will have an emotional feeling that they are close to such a blessed place, which has a significance in our holy scripture as well, so whatever we do good and whatever the learning or the things we are going through, so it's not

> just Allah Almighty who is looking at our activities, but such holy people are lying next to us too that we will have a blessing from as well.

Dr Qadri (2015) recalled how 'in the history of Islam we have that concept, of having a Shrine and sacred places'. The Ka'aba, the first dedicated 'House of God', in the Al-Masjid al-Haram Mosque in Makkah is a sacred place. One of the five pillars of Islam is that Muslims are required to undertake a hajj pilgrimage, at least once in their lifetime to circumambulate the Ka'aba. The most sacred Islamic shrine is the grave of the Prophet Muhammad in the Al-Masjid al-Nabawi Mosque of the Prophet in Madinah. Dr Qadri (2015) also told of how,

> in our Holy Scriptures... there was one event, a couple of pious people, they were lying down in a cave and they died there and there is a complete statement in the Quran, [to] bury them with respect, and make good beautiful shrines, on the grave so that their lives can be remembered and that these people could be role models for the next coming generations. So that is a complete beautiful message there. That's why all those pious people and religious figures, so, their places and graves, are made beautiful monuments, so that they are remembered... So that people, even the generations coming next they're passing by, they will see a very beautiful building and then they will walk in and then they will try to learn who this person was, and through that they will study about him, and then later on, maybe 1000 years after his death, they will be learning from his life. So that's kind of a concept we have, [for] such shrines.

Dr Qadri (2015) stated that in addition to the moral lessons to be learned from the role model's life, there was 'a beautiful concept' of Khanqah where the pious Sufis, the saints, later in life, once they had received their education would move to rural, poor areas, and establish places where they could engage in contemplative practices and also feed and educate the local villagers. He described the 'whole complex' of the Khanqah as a 'spiritual well' providing food and shelter for those in need. When these Sufis died, they were typically buried in these places, which then became shrines. Their sons, and students continued to teach and carry out welfare activities in these places, and people would come to visit and pray there. Dr Qadri (2015) said, 'that's how those shrines and sacred places established into great institutions... that had a very great impact socially on the people'.

One of the most popular shrines in Lahore is Data Darbar, a mausoleum for the great Persian Sufi saint Abul Hassan Ali Hajvari, who migrated from Afghanistan to Pakistan in the eleventh century. Dr Qadri (2015) described this shrine as 'the most sacred place in Lahore'. He estimated that more than 50,000 people in need received food from there per day. He explained how people would regularly visit the shrine to say prayers and to donate money for food for the poor. He added, 'it is a very well-known fact that in the whole of Lahore, that if somebody is hungry, you go to Data Darbar... that has been continuing for 1,000 years, can you imagine that?'

When asked what motivates the people to donate this food at the shrine sites, Dr Qadri (2015) answered that only a very small part of the Quran focuses on humans' relationship with God, while most of it is centred on how humans should behave with other humans. He elaborated that the Quran in particular stresses the need 'to take care of the poor and of orphans' and that if a person refuses to do so, they have 'completely rejected the religion of Islam, by pushing away a hungry, an orphan from his door'. Dr Qadri (2015) explained that 'people know clearly that the biggest worship act, is to feed the hungry in our religion… and… to take care of the orphan… that's a moral obligation'. He described how there was a beautiful story in the Quran of a man facing God on the day of judgement, saying 'God I was performing these good acts, so why you are still angry at me?' God replied 'you remember that day I came to your house and I was hungry and you didn't feed me?' The man could not recall that day and stated, 'God how is it possible, you never came to my house?' To which God responded 'that orphan, or that hungry man who came to your house and asked for food, that was me, and you didn't help me'. Dr Qadri (2015) noted how 'just sitting and remembering [God] won't make God happy with you… God will be only happy with you once you help God's people. That's a basic concept.'

Mr Mash'hadi (2015) similarly described how,

> in Islam or in the religion of Islam, a sacred place is always… linked to a sacred prophet, to a saint or somebody who has been holy, who was a man of God. Now, why did he, how did he become sacred? In the whole of Islamic history, I cannot find any sacred person who has not served the humanity, and God. I can think of people who have been very pious but they have not become sacred… A Sufi becomes sacred when that Sufi benefits humanity. He cannot be a Sufi who is only good with the God, or who is only pious, who only prays all the time. The constitution of a Sufi or a saint is based on serving humanity.

Mr Mash'hadi (2015) also stated that,

> in Islam, giving charity is one of the five basic principles of the religion. It is compulsory… if a Muslim does the four but doesn't do charity work, especially when they can afford it, is not following the religion of Islam properly. So it's one of the basic pillars of Islam.

Dr Qadri (2015) mentioned another tradition, derived from the scriptures, 'that if somebody is in stress, somebody is in any pressure, any crisis, the biggest act to get yourself out of that crisis is to feed people'. He said that charity is recommended as 'the solution to every crisis'. So whenever people face personal difficulties, such as family, business or health troubles, or stresses such as passing an exam, they go to Data Darbar or another shrine, to pray to God and to donate food there for hundreds or thousands of people. This also generates significant employment opportunities for the cooks and shopkeepers at these shrines. The shrines are also sites for additional welfare activities, such as providing education in adjacent schools, and medical assistance in adjacent hospitals. Dr Qadri (2015) noted that some of these shrines, these institutions have been undertaking these development activities for 'thousands and thousands of years... so that's a major contribution'.

Mr Mash'hadi (2015) also reflected on,

> why do the people come to the shrines? They come to these shrines to pay their respect, but also, to get the blessing for themselves... many of the people they... distribute food to the people who can't afford food. The concept of that is they go to those places, they will feed the poor people, and the God will be happy with that and God will help them solve their problems... help[ing] the poor people, help[ing] the needy people... makes God happy and God then gives a solution to the problems of that individual... once the concept is clear, then it becomes very easy to understand the concept of charity which evolves around these shrines, which evolves around these Sufis and saints.

Mr Mash'hadi (2015) stated that the Aghosh Orphanage and school were constructed beside the Shaykh Tahir Alauddin Al-Qadri shrine and provide a high quality education to their students. This shrine is also a major site of the Qurbani food distribution programme and of monthly gatherings where 5,000–7,000 people are not only fed, but also attend spiritual teachings to guide their daily conduct.

Mr Mash'hadi (2015) explained how according to Islamic principles, traditionally when an animal is slaughtered its meat is divided into three parts; one part is for personal use, the second is for relatives who are in need of assistance, and the third is for the poor who cannot afford to buy and slaughter an animal. In the case of the Qurbani programme, however, most people who pay for the slaughter of the animal distribute this meat entirely to the poor, and do not keep any of it, even though they have that option. Mr Mash'hadi (2015) added how people in richer countries often chose to send their Qurbani packages to people in poorer nations.

Mr Mash'hadi (2015) further described how MQI's, MES's and MWF's emphasis on education is an integral part of charity and sustainability.

> If somebody's asking for charity today, or [if] somebody's hands are empty today, we, the concept and ideology is that we deliver something to them in a way that tomorrow these hands become the one which *give* not take... the concept of charity is not only food... but it is also giving proper awareness, spiritual awareness. Teachings, education... once a person, once an individual is given awareness... [on] how he has to spend his life [helping others], that sometimes is better than serving food for one day... charity, in a greater sense, is educating a child today. If he is a child today, being educated, tomorrow he will be somebody who will support his family [and community]... [this is of much] greater benefit, [and a] much greater output of that charity work.

Dr Qadri (2015) clarified that mosques, which were often found adjacent to shrines, were places of worship, but that they were not places for welfare activities. He also stated that while some MQI schools were built near existing shrines or mosques, their schools typically only included prayer rooms and that MQI didn't build new mosques. Mr Mash'hadi (2015) also stated that rather than building mosques, MQI and MWF focused on building 'community centres' which provided a range of activities to benefit local people.

Finally, Dr Qadri (2015) explained how neither he or his father or his grandfather made or currently make a living from their MQI work. His grandfather, ash-Shaykh Dr Farida'd-Din al-Qadri was a trained doctor by profession and 'a great Sufi saint and religious classic scholar by passion'. His father, Shaykh-ul-Islam, was a lawyer and law professor, and Dr Hussain Qadri's brother Dr Hasan Mohi-ud-din Qadri also has a Ph.D. in law. They currently have family businesses from which they generate their incomes and they don't personally earn any money from their MQI activities. Dr Qadri (2015) stated 'no return we accept, or expect in this world against the service we are doing to God and people, that is only solely for people and the happiness of God'. Shaykh-ul-Islam and his sons have faced 'many hurdles and difficulties' and also have 'many enemies' who are threatened by their actions. There have been many assassination attempts on them and their families and over a dozen attacks in which lives have been lost, yet the motivation to keep helping others, 'to make our Lord and God happy' keeps them strong in the face of this opposition and danger.

Conclusion

Shrines of Sufi saints are the main sacred places around which MQI, MES and MWF conduct their development activities. As described above, the teachings of the Prophet Muhammad (SAW) and the lives of these Sufi masters, Shaykh-ul-Islam and his sons, serve as inspirations for charitable acts that enable MQI's welfare initiatives.

The enormous scope of MQI activities is virtually completely dependent on the generosity of those who offer service and donations to the organisation in order to feed the poor and to assist orphans and others in need. This charity is an essential pillar of Islam that is embodied in the lives of the saints who serve as role models to the people, and in the shrines that are dedicated to them.

Following in the footsteps of notable saints, MQI leaders have been and continue to face persecution for calling existing power structures into account on issues of justice, equality and distribution of resources. Their calls for social and political change have been inspired by Islamic principles and their actions have taken place in sacred places often intensifying their potency, given their significance not only to MQI but to the population of Lahore and the wider Pakistani and global Muslim community.

MQI, MES and MWF's community centres and schools in rural locations, whether established beside existing mosques or shrines or not, follow the traditional way in which Sufi masters have long conducted their outreach activities. It is quite possible that these places will become future sacred sites, and that the leaders, staff and volunteers of MQI, MES and MWF will be recognised as future Sufi saints, given their beneficial work for humanity.

Notes

1 In this chapter we have used the spelling, acronyms and titles provided on the Minhaj-ul-Quran International's (MQI) websites' English versions, and by Dr Hussain Mohi-ud-Din Qadri.
2 A detailed analyses of PAT's political activities is beyond the scope of this chapter, which is primarily concerned with MQI's sacred places and development activities although it recognises that the two are interrelated given PAT's emphasis on providing economic stability, justice, gender equity and human rights.
3 Dr Hussain Mohi-ud-Din Qadri was interviewed for this case study and allowed his comments to be identified in this chapter. They are cited as (Qadri 2015), as the interview was conducted in 2015.
4 Mr Dawood Mash'hadi was interviewed for this case study and allowed his comments to be identified in this chapter. They are cited as (Mash'hadi 2015), as the interview was conducted in 2015.

References

Gosha-e-Durood (GeD) n.d.a, *About-Gosha-e-Durood*, viewed 10 Feb 2015, http://www.gosha-e-durood.com/english/tid/16131/About-Gosha-e-Durood.html.

Gosha-e-Durood (GeD) n.d.b, *Minara-tus-Salam (Gosha-e-Durood) building*, viewed 10 February 2015, http://www.gosha-e-durood.com/english/tid/23050.

Itikaf City n.d.a, *About*, viewed 10 February 2015, http://www.itikaf.com/english/tid/14303/itikaf-city-by-minhaj-ul-quran-international.html.

Itikaf City n.d.b, *Contact us*, viewed 10 February 2015, http://www.itikaf.com/english/tid/14324/contact-details-itikaf-city-of-minhaj-ul-quran.html.

Minhaj-ul-Quran International (MQI) n.d.a, *A profile of Shaykh-ul-Islam Dr Muhammad Tahir-ul-Qadri*, viewed 10 February 2015, http://www.minhaj.org/english/tid/8718/A-Profile-of-Shaykh-ul-Islam-Dr-Muhammad-Tahir-ul-Qadri.html.

Minhaj-ul-Quran International (MQI) n.d.b, *About, Introduction, Minhaj-ul-Quran-International*, viewed 10 February 2015, http://www.minhaj.org/english/tid/1799/Minhaj-ul-Quran-International.html.

Minhaj Welfare Foundation (MWF) n.d.a, *About*, viewed 10 February 2015, http://www.welfare.org.pk/english/tid/8723/About-MWF.html.

Minhaj Welfare Foundation (MWF) n.d.b, *Aghosh orphan care*, viewed 10 February 2015, http://www.welfare.org.pk/english/tid/3533/Aghosh-%28Orphan-Care-Home%29.html.

Minhaj Welfare Foundation (MWF) n.d.c, *Ongoing projects*, viewed 10 February 2015, http://www.welfare.org.pk/english/tid/24681/Ongoing-Projects.html.

Minhaj Welfare Foundation (MWF) n.d.d, *Qurbani program*, viewed 10 February 2015, http://www.welfare.org.pk/english/tid/34221/Minhaj-Welfare-Foundation-Qurbani-Program-2015-meat-distribution-poor-people-refugees.html.

Shaykh-ul-IslamDr Muhammad Tahir-ul-Qadri 2011, *Profile of Shaykh-ul-Islam*, viewed 10 February 2015, http://www.drtahirulqadri.com/main/profile-of-shaykh-ul-islam.

4 Songdhammakalyani Monastery and gender equity in modern Buddhism[1]

Introduction

Arriving in Bangkok, the humidity is striking, as is the contrast between the lush tropical vegetation, the industrialised landscape and the many shrines and temples, large and small that can be seen driving on the highway to Songdhammakalyani Monastery (SDKM). The road is lined with many car yards, furniture display rooms, billboards for new homes, McDonalds, Starbucks, high-rise flats and smaller local businesses. The giant three-headed elephant statue, atop of the Erawan Museum of Thai antiques and Buddhist cosmology, is an arresting sight and frangipanis and lotuses bloom in gardens and ponds on the way. Thankfully, the traffic moves quickly bypassing Bangkok city, its silhouette visible through light smog in the distance.

Approaching Nakhonpathom, a seemingly economically poorer area, the buildings are typically only one to two stories high and the number of temples and smaller golden roadside shrines increase, decorated with flowers. On the right is the Large Golden Buddha, SDKM's landmark, recognisable from the directions provided on the Monastery's website.

Pulling into the SDKM complex it is much larger than expected, with a three-story Uposatha Hall on one side beside the golden Buddha and a kindergarten, organic garden and large three-storey Yasodhara Vihara on the other. The humble ground floor office contains a small but impressive collection of books in Thai and English, many written by Dhammananda Bhikkhuni the Monastery's Abbess, and of *Yasodhara* newsletters, which Ven. Dhammananda has produced since the mid-1980s.

Walking toward the three-story accommodation block of rooms for visitors, it's evident that there are many buildings here in this large Monastery. All of the buildings are well-constructed and maintained, with building works continuing and piles of materials relatively neatly stacked under and beside the guest quarters. The guest rooms each have two single beds, a ceiling fan, a clothes rack and a private bathroom. They have orange speckled marble lino floors, light green walls, louvered windows and balconies overlooking the temple gardens and sacred Bodhi tree. There's a constant hum of traffic from the Petkasem Highway on one side, bird and insect songs from treetops coming from the other, and a whizzing sound from the ceiling fan above. On the outskirts of urban Bangkok, tradition and modernity coexist in everyday life and spaces.

Morning chanting at SDKM begins at 5.30 a.m. The bell rings at 5.20, and the dogs that protect the Monastery begin to howl. The seven fully ordained bhikkhunis, five sikkhamanas (nuns in training to be bhikkhunis), and two samaneris (novice nuns) form one line on the right side of the ground floor of the Uposatha Hall, and the maechee (similar to samaneri but lay people in white robes), volunteers and visitors form another on the left. Both lines bow to the many gold statues of Buddhas and Buddhist teachers decorated with high-quality plastic flowers. The room is dimly lit.

The bhikkhunis and nuns then turn around and file up one flight of stairs while the second line files up another. At the top of these stairs, both lines bow to a large golden Buddha statue, and towards the bedroom where Bhikkhuni Ta Tao, Venerable Dhammananda's mother, spent the final years of her life. Opposite this room is the chanting space, which has pews upon which the bhikkhunis and nuns sit facing more golden and clay Buddhas of different sizes. There is also a glass cabinet of relics, encased in miniature stupas. There are also pictures on the walls of Buddhas and Bodhisattvas, male and female. The bhikkhunis and nuns sit at the front and the maechees, volunteers and visitors, at the back. When Ven. Dhammananda joins the chanting sessions she sits even further back beside the door.

The bhikkhunis and nuns bow to the Buddhas and chant for 30 minutes as the sun rises. These include offering prayers of light, incense and flowers, which have already been placed beside the main Buddha statue, and praises to the Buddha, Dhamma and Sangha. The bhikkhunis and nuns also chant protection prayers, the Buddha's first teaching after enlightenment, and prayers to the eight male saints.

After the chanting, if Ven. Dhammananda has been in the session, she leaves the room before anyone else. The bhikkhunis and nuns then file up one set of stairs to the top floor Meditation Hall, and the maechees, volunteers and visitors another. Once again there are a retinue of Buddhas and Bodhisattvas and a life-size photograph of Bhikkhuni Ta Tao draped in beautiful flowers. Meditation begins with a chant by the bhikkhunis and nuns who sit in the front, with maechees, volunteers and visitors behind them, and also lasts for 30 minutes. A balcony door is open and many fans are on, to cope with the heat. The traffic noise is very loud in this room, but the sound of birds singing their morning songs is still audible. The traffic doesn't seem to bother the bhikkhunis and nuns in the slightest.

A similar chanting ritual is conducted every evening for 45 minutes as the sun sets. This includes offering prayers of light, incense and flowers, which were earlier placed beside the main Buddha statue, and praises to the Buddha, Dhamma and Sangha. The nuns recite refuge chants, the Noble Eightfold Path, prayers on death and impermanence, prayers for forgiveness and praises to the thirteen Arahat Theris, bhikkhunis who were praised by the Buddha for their great abilities.

The bhikkhunis and nuns also engage in an afternoon communal working session in which they may weed or attend to the gardens, or clean the temples and statues, especially in preparation for public events. The bhikkhunis and nuns also participate in daily Dhamma study sessions led by Ven. Dhammananda in the library, which overlooks the main temple on one side and the Bodhi tree garden on another. Breakfasts and lunches are served on the second floor of the Yasodhara Temple building in a large hall below the third story, which houses statues of the thirteen Arahat Theris. The bhikkhunis and nuns say prayers for about ten minutes before each meal to bless the food, which is offered by the volunteers. Once a week three bhikkhunis are chosen to conduct an alms round in the streets around the Monastery. They are accompanied by a volunteer with a cart to carry the generous amount of food offered by local families and businesses. The bhikkhunis and nuns stop at their houses and factories and bestow them with prayers and blessings. They also conduct community outreach activities at a local detention centre for young men and a women's prison. These are their main development activities.

Thai bhikkhunis

Ven. Dhammananda,[2] formerly known as Chatsumarn Kabilsingh, is a world renowned Thai bhikkhuni and widely published scholar, who has dedicated her life to campaigning for full ordination and respect for Buddhist women. Ven. Dhammananda follows in the footsteps of her mother Ven. Voramai Kabilsingh, who was given the title Bhikkhuni Ta Tao when she took higher ordination in Taiwan in 1971.

The life stories of these two remarkable women, and the history of bhikkhuni ordination and controversy surrounding it, are crucial to understanding the sacred places of SDKM and the development activities of the bhikkhunis who founded it and who reside here. Their work must also be understood within the context of the international Buddhist women's social movement and their quest for gender equity in global Buddhism. The Monastery's website forms part of the Buddhist women's social movement online network that is expanding the reach and impact of their activities internationally. These online sacred spaces will also be briefly examined in this chapter.

Lamai Kabilsingh was born in Rajburi, approximately 100 kilometres west of Bangkok in 1908. Soon after she was born, her father abandoned her mother and their five daughters, taking their only son with him. Lamai's mother Somcheen raised her daughters in Bangkok, where Lamai attended Assumption Girls' College. She worked in her Chinese brother-in-law's store, which sold foreign food, and it was here that she learned English. She became a schoolteacher, specialising in physical education, and excelled in sword fighting and jujitsu. She also had a life-long interest in literature, writing and journalism (Dhammananda 2014).

Lamai married Korkiat Shatsena in 1942 and changed her name to Voramai. They moved to southern Thailand, where his wealthy family was from, and had one daughter and adopted another. Voramai moved back to Bangkok with her children to provide them with a better education. She sent Chatsumarn to Rajini Bon, the best school in Bangkok. Korkiat Shatsena was a politician and Voramai worked as a journalist reporting on the conflict in Southern Thailand at this time. She witnessed much suffering and poverty while travelling with her husband to remote villages and made 'a heartfelt commitment' (Dhammananda 2014, p. 63) to educating children who were the country's future. She later established a school for orphans, which remained open for three decades (Dhammananda 2014).

In 1954, Voramai was diagnosed with a tumour and hospitalised. One of her sisters brought Maechee Thongsuk to visit her. She was a respected pupil of a famous monk, meditator and healer Luangpo Sod. Voramai made a small donation, as this was all she could give from hospital, and the following day the Maechee returned saying that Luangpo Sod had said there was no longer any need for her to have the operation. Voramai proceeded with the surgery; however, the doctors could no longer find the tumour. Could the monk have truly cured her? Voramai decided to go to study meditation with Luangpo Sod and Maechee Thongsuk at Wat Pakham (Dhammananda 2014). Ven. Dhammananda (2015) explained how before her tumour her mother lived in 'the fast lane' and wasn't religious at all, however after Voramai was cured she became highly committed and studied diligently. Ven. Dhammananda (2015) was eight years old when her mother first began to meditate and she would sometimes practice with her. She recalled the impact this had on her later development.

> ... she would get up early, like 5 o'clock and she would be meditating, under a mosquito net... and I would be sleeping next to her, she would wake me up and both of us would be sitting, and after that she'd close her eyes and I would crawl down to sleep again [laughs]... But that... kind of gives you early training and early access to meditation and it becomes part of you.
>
> (Dhammananda 2015)

Voramai soon earned the title Dhammakaya, which meant she could now teach Dhamma and meditation practices to others. She began to publish *Vipassana Bantherngsarn*, a monthly magazine of Buddhist teachings in 1955, that she continued publishing for 32 years (Dhammananda 2014).

On 2 May 1956 Voramai was ordained by bhikkhu Chao Kun Pra Prommuni, the Deputy Abbot of Wat Bavornnives, but not as a bhikkuni given that people were told that bhikkhuni ordination was impossible in Thailand, as the bhikkhuni lineage had died out. While she wore white on her ordination day, she decided to wear light yellow robes instead of the white maechee robe following her ordination. This caused a stir initially, however the Sangha Council of Elders, of which Chao Kun Pra Prommuni was a respected member, decided that as the colour she had chosen was different to the one the monks wore they could not see that she would cause the Sangha any harm (Dhammananda 2014).

Many young women were drawn to her and Voramai formed a nun's community. Inspired by the Catholic nuns she had known while studying at Assumption College, Voramai taught her nuns to be self-sufficient. They founded a stone factory making soapstone utensils and other handicrafts (Dhammananda 2014).

According to Ven. Dhammananda (2014, p. 67), '[t]he idea of building a temple for bhikkhunis had been with Voramai since the beginning'. Legally she had to buy six rai of land to start a temple, so she did so 50 kilometres outside of Bangkok. She founded SDKM and began to build an Uposatha Hall, a shrine room where the Sangha practices could be conducted, which took ten years to finish (Dhammananda 2014). Voramai also built a relatively humble residential building for the first nuns, which she dedicated to her own mother, Ven. Dhammananda's grandma, or yaai in Thai (Dhammananda 2015).

At this time, Chatsumarn was completing her academic studies in Canada and had learned that it was possible to be ordained as a bhikkhuni in Taiwan. Voramai and Chatsumarn travelled to Taipei in 1971 and Voramai's bhikkhuni ordination was conferred in a special ceremony by her preceptor bhikkhu Tao An Fashih of Sung San Temple, and twelve other bhikkhus. She was given the name Bhikkhuni Ta Tao, yet continued to be called Voramai. She returned to her Monastery, and focused on Dhamma teachings, in written and spoken form. She also became widely known as a healer following in the footsteps of her first master (Dhammananda 2014).

Bhikkhuni ordination – high ordination for Buddhism women – is a controversial topic internationally, given that it is not yet recognised by male Buddhist leaders in some countries, including Thailand. Chatsumarn continued along her academic path and participated at a 1983 Conference on Religion and Social Changes at Harvard University, to speak on 'the future of the Bhikkhuni Sangha in Thailand' at the request of then Dr Diana Eck, who is now a world-leading Professor and expert on religious pluralism and peacebuilding. Dhammananda (2007, p. 75) cites this as a turning point in her becoming 'more committed to the work of Buddhist women' as it was 'an eye opening conference' that made her 'socially aware' of her position as a scholar and daughter of a Thai bhikkhuni. After the conference she realised it was 'not sufficient to sit in the ivory tower' when she was the foremost expert on bhikkhunis in Thailand, given her Ph.D. was on this topic and her and her mother's direct experiences. She began reaching out to other Buddhist women and founded the International Buddhist Women's Activities Newsletter in 1984, which later became *Yasodhara*.

Chatsumarn became one of the founding members of a Buddhist women's social movement Sakyadhita, the International Association of Buddhist Women that has campaigned for gender equality in global Buddhism since the late 1980s. Another of Sakyadhita's founders, Ven. Ayya Khema, a German nun who also spent a lot of time in Australia, established a training centre for nuns on Parapaduwa Island in southern Sri Lanka in 1984. Ven. Karma Lekshe Tsomo, an American Tibetan Buddhist nun who was working in India at that time, had the idea of organising the first international conference for Buddhist nuns at Bodhgaya, the place of Buddha's enlightenment. Chatsumarn, Ayya Khema, Venerable Jampa Tsedroen and the Venerable Thubten Chodron all assisted Venerable Karma Lekshe Tsomo to hold the event after His Holiness the Dalai Lama's annual talk in February 1987. His Holiness attended the opening ceremony and 200 delegates from 26 countries participated in the conference. Sakyadhita arose from this first conference, and the next Conference on Buddhist Women was held at Thammasat University in Bangkok in 1991, and organised by Chatsumarn. She was elected Sakyadhita President at this conference and held this office until 1995 (Dhammananda 2007).

Ven. Dhammananda (2015) explained how in the mid-1990s she stepped away from Sakyadhita to focus more on her own commitments in Thailand.

> Ah yes I started Sakyadhita way back in 1987, as one of the three co-founders, I was with them until 1995. Then I slip out because I was preparing for my own ordination, my own commitment, which for me was more important... I step out and focus more on building the bhikkhunis on this soil. So, moving from my involvement as an academic... to be committed, how to make that topic that we are talking as academics into reality... I turn my attention, my commitment, to actually be on the ground and make a reality for Thailand. Then when I feel a bit settled, then I again return to Sakyadhita... as a participant.
>
> (Dhammananda 2015)

In 2001, Chatsumarn took samaneri (novice) precepts in Sri Lanka and received the name Dhammananda. A year later Bhikkhuni Ta Tao, at the age of 94 told her daughter, 'I am leaving' (Dhammananda 2014, p. 69). Ven. Dhammananda joked that her mother couldn't leave yet as Ven. Dhammananda was only a samaneri. Bhikkhuni Ta Tao nodded and waited. Ven. Dhammananda received full bhikkhuni ordination in Sri Lanka in February 2003 and Bhikkhuni Ta Tao passed away peacefully aged 95, on June 24, that same year. Soon after, six bhikkhunis arrived from Sri Lanka, Indonesia and Vietnam, and spent the three-month rains retreat (vassa) at SDKM under the instruction of Bhikkhuni Rahatungoda Saddha Sumana. For the first time in Thailand's history, the bhikhunni patimokkha (code of discipline) was recited during the 2003 vassa (Dhammananda 2014).

Sakyadhita has continued to hold regular conferences on average every two years throughout Asia. In recent years the Buddhist women's social movement has expanded and conducted activism digitally through Sakyadhita (n.d.), the Alliance for Bhikkhunis (n.d.), the Yogini Project (n.d) websites, Facebook pages and Twitter accounts, as part of the rise of global digital activism supporting processes of democratisation and peacebuilding (Tomalin et al. 2015). SDKM (n.d.) also has a website linked to this network which promotes its and the broader Thai Bhikkhuni Sangha's activities.

SDKM has continued to grow as women of diverse ages and backgrounds are drawn to Ven. Dhammananda's teachings. One of the bhikkhunis working there, Ven. Dhammavanna,[3] recounted how she had memories of seeing the Golden Buddha as a child.

> … when I was ten years old I always go travelling to another province… we always saw that big Buddha statue… but we didn't know what is this place… the bhikkhuni place, we didn't know at all.
>
> (Dhammavanna 2015)

Later, when Ven. Dhammavanna was a first year university student, Dhammananda was one of her lecturers and she was really impressed with her teaching, finding her to be very inspiring. Ven. Dhammavanna completed her course and became a journalist but found it very stressful. A health crisis, which caused her severe back pain, led her to seek out Ven. Dhammananda to help lift her spirits and deepen her Buddhist practice. She found out that the nearby temple with the Golden Buddha was in fact Ven. Dhammananda's Monastery. Ven. Dhammavanna recalled her first impressions of visiting SDKM as a young adult and the steps she took towards bhikkhuni ordination and to healing her body and mind with Ven. Dhammananda's guidance.

> At first I came here… at the time I'm so weak, I'm not have energy, to help myself, to lift up, to anything. And I came here like this is ten year ago [laughs]. I have my back pain… At that time I'm only 29 years old and when Dhammananda asks 'What do you do with your life? Why are you so like this?' and I ask to stay here for seven days… And she say yes… And it's helped me, to… develop myself. You will see in the evening, we working together, even though I can not do anything so much. But it helps… to get me better…Yes, and also when we chanting, I love chanting. It will be healing… healing time. Even though the mediation also is help. And I decide to resign from my job, because of… after I go back, my heart not there. I thought, is the time for me to go in this ordained path, to the monastic.
>
> (Dhammavanna 2015)

At first Ven. Dhammavanna worked on the reception desk and then began to take care of the Monastery's accounts and to manage donations. After one month she was permitted to take her first eight precepts, shave her head and to stay on at SDKM where her health continued to improve. After a year she was able to receive the novice samaneri ordination, and after three years the sikhamuna ordination in preparation for becoming a bhikkhuni. Ven. Dhammavanna was very grateful for this experience.

> … when I look back, I feel proud, I feel thankful for when the Dhammananda teaching me. I thought, right now, no one have this best type of teaching. Even though when you receive the teaching, for the teacher is not easy, is hard. Is painful. But if you can accept, if you can consider… is the practice,

> is very good practice… Yeah. Not easy to be a good monk… But the discipline will protect you.
>
> (Dhammavanna 2015)

One of the novice nuns, Shirley,[4] who was originally from Malaysia, also explained how she came to be at SDKM.

> I was already retired, and back home there was nothing else to do other than going to high tea, wasting money, going everywhere with my friends, sometimes we go drinking in the evening, karaoke, so my family was a little bit worried… especially my mum and my brother, we are very close. So my mum was thinking 'why don't you just go somewhere and do some learning?' So I say 'no I'm too old for learning! Then my brother say, 'there's a temple in Thailand, they have all female monks', because I like to pray, I'm a born Buddhist… So he says, 'why don't you just go over there and do some retreats and do meditation and check this out… [you're] wasting your time at home'. And so I was thinking… ok, ok, ok, I go… Just for one month.
>
> (Shirley 2015)

After a month, and despite many obstacles she decided to ordain as a samaneri. However, at the first Monastery Shirley lived in they didn't speak English, only Thai, so it was difficult for her to further her monastic education and deepen her practice. Instead she worked in the Monastery's café, where she enjoyed making cappuccinos and helping to sell coffee to support her community, but felt frustrated as she wasn't learning enough. As she explained, 'you read your own books to keep learning. [But] I want a teacher, I want interaction you see' (Shirley 2015). After encountering many more challenges she was finally able to come to SDKM to study with Ven. Dhammananda, who she knew to be a learned bhikkhuni who taught in English.

> I'm very happy here. Every day she teaches English… she writes on the board in English but explains in Thai… And I get to learn my Dhamma learning in English… Every day, I'm happy. I'm so happy sweeping the floor. You don't get disturbance, it's so peaceful here. You got time for work, time for play, time for sleep right. So it's like, I'm so happy… Dhammananda is the very best Principal.
>
> (Shirley 2015)

Both Ven. Dhammavanna and Shirley displayed the highest respect for their teacher and were very happy and content with their life in the Monastery.

Countering gender inequity in Buddhism

Ongoing debates about bhikkhuni ordination date back to the time of the Buddha. Buddha's wife and later pupil Yasodhara, his stepmother and later pupil Maha Pajapati and the thirteen female Arahat Theris, bhikkhunis who were praised by Buddha for their foremost powers, are all embodied in SDKM's sacred places, as are Bhikkhuni Ta Tao and Bhikkhuni Dhammananda.

Buddhism is one of the world's largest religions, with a high degree of popularity in Western societies, yet long-standing issues regarding gender inequality remain within it. The vast majority of Buddhist archetypes of enlightenment remain male and positions of power within Buddhist organisations continue to be largely held by men (Tsomo 2009). This is a human rights and development issue given that gender disparities continue to persist in Buddhist societies, linked to cultural and religious beliefs and practices, which allocate a lower status to women (Tomalin et al. 2015; Owen 1998). Sakyadhita, and other Buddhist women's organisations and networks including SDKM, continue to support women and men from diverse traditions in their quest for greater acceptance of full ordination, various types of training, educational opportunities, and improved standards of living for Buddhist nuns and women, particularly in economically poorer societies (Sakyadhita n.d.; Fenn and Koppedrayer 2008, p. 55).

Ven. Dhammananda is one of the leading scholars of gender and Buddhism internationally, who reminds us that the Buddha ordained male bhikkhus and female bhikkhunis in his lifetime, despite his initial resistance to this idea. Buddha's stepmother Maha Pajapati, who had raised him after his mother's untimely death a week after his birth, was the first woman to request ordination from the Buddha. He is said to have refused her three times without providing a reason. Ananda, one of the Buddha's disciples, then asked Buddha on Maha Pajapati's behalf, and the Buddha refuted him also again with no explanation. Ananda asked whether Buddha had refused them on the basis that women couldn't reach enlightenment to which the Buddha replied unequivocally that women could become enlightened and then finally agreed to ordain Maha Pajapati (Dhammananda 2007). Ven. Dhammananda (2007, p. 18) has stated that '[i]t was purely because of this equal spiritual ability that the Buddha allowed women to join the Sangha' and that '[t]his acceptance can and should be taken as a golden phrase for uplifting Buddhist women'.

Buddha is said to have agreed to ordain Maha Pajapati on the condition that she followed an additional eight conditions (garudhammas) that monks were not, and still are not, required to follow (Dhammananda 2007; Tsomo 2009). These instructions which were apparently given to protect the bhikkhunis and the Sangha remain contentious given that they, alongside many other controversial references from Buddhist texts, discriminate against women and are often cited as the underlying causes of gender inequality in Buddhism (Gross 1993). Yet some scholars argue that the eight conditions may not have been actually imposed by the Buddha but rather added subsequently by his followers (Tsomo 2009; Kustiani 2013).

The other main reason that is frequently given against female ordination in Buddhism is the claim that the bhikkhuni lineage has died out and that both bhikkhunis and bhikkhus need to be present to legitimise a bhikkhuni ordination, so there is no way of restoring this lineage. Ven. Dhammananda (2007) has explained how the Buddha allowed bhikkhus to ordain bhikkhunis and also for dual ordination so this should not be a concern, and while Buddhism was established without bhikkhunis in Thailand, Burma and Tibet, the bhikkhuni lineage was maintained in Taiwan and reestablished in Sri Lanka and China. Since then bhikkhuni lineages have been established in Indonesia, Thailand and Vietnam (Dhammananda 2007). More recently, Venerable Ajahn Brahm has ordained bhikkhuni in the Thai Forest tradition in Western Australia and these events have generated significant controversy in Thailand and also online.

Buddhism, like most major religious traditions is full of internal debates on this and other issues. What can be agreed upon with no doubt is that Buddha ordained women as bhikkhunis, and that whatever cultural frameworks affected the way he did so, or affected the way that subsequent Sangha perceived them, these bhikkhunis are equally as capable as men to reach enlightenment. What is also beyond doubt is that bhikkhunis make up one of the crucial aspects of the Fourfold Buddhists on which the future of Buddhism depends (Dhammananda 2007). Ven. Dhammananda (2007, p. 25) explained that the Buddha stated that for Buddhism to prosper in future the Fourfold Buddhists, that is bhikkhus, bhikkhunis, lay men and lay women, must 'respect the Buddha, the Dhamma [teachings of the Buddha], the Sangha [monastic community], Sikkha (monastic code) and Samadhi (meditation or practice)'. The Buddha also said that for a country to be a central Buddhist country it must have all Fourfold Buddhists. Ven. Dhammananda (2007, p. 25) thereby concludes that the 'establishment of bhikkhuni Sangha is a sign of a prosperous [Buddhist] community' and should be encouraged, not resisted.

Moreover, during Buddha's lifetime there were thirteen bhikkhuni that were named and praised for being foremost in their abilities. These women were: Maha Pajapati Gotami Arahat Theri, Buddha's stepmother, foremost as long-standing bhikkhuni; Khema Arahat Theri, foremost in wisdom; Uppalavanna Arahat Theri, foremost in performing miracles; Patacala Arahat Theri, foremost in monastic discipline; Dhammadinna Arahat Theri, foremost in giving Dhamma; Nanda Arahat Theri, foremost in Jhanic practice; Sona Arahat Theri, foremost in endurance; Sakula Arahat Theri, foremost in having divine eyes; Kundalakesi Arahat Theri, foremost in quick wisdom; Bhadda Kapilani Arahat Theri, foremost in remembering past lives; Bhadda Kaccana, Yasodhara, Buddha's wife, Arahat Theri, foremost in supernatural performances; Kisa Gotami Arahat Theri, foremost in wearing course robe; and Singalamata Arahat Theri, foremost in practicing through faith. The altar of the top floor of the Yasodhara Vihara, named after one of the thirteen Arahat Theris and Buddha's wife, at SDKM has large golden statues of these thirteen bhikkhuni including inscriptions of their names and their abilities, with Maha Pajapati in the central highest space. Beside the altar is a large photograph of Bhikkhuni Ta Tao and beside her a statue of the Buddha adorned with flowers.

Most of the thirteen bhikkhuni came from privileged backgrounds, but many also experienced hardships including tragic deaths of children, husbands and parents, poverty, neglect, betrayal, abandonment and madness before being ordained, and even one incident of rape after ordination. Two of the women were particularly attached to their beauty before being taught by the Buddha that all will inevitably succumb to old age. All of these women renounced their possessions, became bhikkhunis and studied the Dhamma (Dhammananda 2012). All were highly accomplished and now serve as role models to new generations of aspiring bhikkhunis. The statues of the thirteen Arahat Theris look over and protect the Monastery and the bhikkhunis and female volunteers and guests who reside within it.

Songdhammakalyani Monastery's sacred places

When asked about SDKM's sacred places, Ven. Dhammananda (2015) explained how traditional rituals had to be conducted to consecrate the place for the Uposatha Hall 'to become a sacred ground' where bhikkhuni ordination and other ceremonies and practices could take place. Ven. Dhammananda thought that the original ceremony her mother conducted to consecrate the land was incorrect and so she conducted a second one. Ven. Dhammananda also acquired another three adjoining rai to extend the Monastery. She described the third floor meditation space of the Uposatha Hall as 'the most sacred place in this whole Monastery', recalling how,

> one time Venerable Grandma said as she was in meditation, she said the roof was gone... She couldn't see the roof. But on each column, there were devas, all of them in meditating position...so she always tell us that when you come up, you don't see anything, but you have to know that the devas, the Angels, use this space to come and meditate. So you have to pay respect to the place.
>
> (Dhammananda 2015)

The Uposatha Hall where the nuns chant and practice their meditation is right beside the highway so the noise can initially be an issue, which is gradually overcome. As Ven. Dhammavanna (2015) stated:

> Normally, normally, everyone will come here and...complain [laugh] about the noise or the road... But maybe, I used to, about the noise... is not trouble me. Not disturb me at all. For I myself... something that disturb me is not the surrounding, but your mind.
>
> (Dhammavanna 2015)

Shirley (2015) had a similar story to tell:

> ... actually when I first came, I also think about the noises outside highway, but as we come in and stay, and during meditation when we are up there, Dhammananda says if you hear the thing just let it go, ohh it's so noisy, just let it go. At the end when you practice and then you cultivate, make your

> mind positive, you actually, it doesn't disturb you at all. This morning outside I heard noises, but it doesn't, as you stay along here... the noise is there yes, but you can just let it go...
>
> (Shirley 2015)

Shirley (2015) also described how being at SDKM had given her the space and ability to slow down, and train her mind in meditation, to be a better and happier person.

> ... when actually you're chanting and you do meditation it's like, it's already in you, already in you, so when it's time to do meditation you just sit down, we're actually... train[ing] our mind to be focused, so it's like, whatever comes, let it go, whatever comes. So for me, I learned one thing, happiness will come but they don't stay, they will go. Suffering will come, but they also don't stay, they will go. So, whatever comes, let go. Then you will be a happier person... We have attachment because we are human. So we have to practice that you know. I think that I am 40 percent better than I was not here... I learned to let go a lot of things, sufferings. I still have a lot to learn... right now here... I'm actually training myself to tone down myself... So I'm getting better and better... I like to do things fast. But now here, no. Even eating... you must train to sit down, and eat slow... so I'm learning... but it's a happy thing that I'm here. Happy. Happy because, I'm already old, 60, what can I do? You know? But my mind is very clear... I'm toning myself, balancing out myself you know. Too quick... But now I'm, little bit more wisdom. It's all I want from Buddha-wisdom and patience. Wisdom, and patience.

Ven. Dhammananda (2015) described the Yasodhara Temple's third floor, which houses the thirteen Arahat Theris, as the second most sacred space, following the Uposatha Meditation Hall. She explained that,

> this is the very first temple in the whole country that has, that created this space for women. So on gender wise, this would be very important... [The Uposatha] is important for any Buddhist you know... But for us, this is important for us, because it represents a space that we provide for the women. So we also come and we have large group of people, we come and meditate on this side.
>
> (Dhammananda 2015)

Ven. Dhammavanna (2015) recalled how the statues of the thirteen Arahat Theris, offered by a layman who had cast them, initially lived on the ground floor of the Uposatha Hall, but then Ven. Dhammananda decided that they needed to honour the Arahat Theris and build a Vihara to house them, 'to lift them up' and 'pay respect to the bhikkhuni' and also to protect them from floods.

The Yasodhara Vihara is the newest building in the Monastery complex and was quite an undertaking to fundraise for and to build. Ven. Dhammananda's (2015) philosophy of fundraising has two central components – to be a 'good nun' and to develop trust with donors through a reliable and impressive track record. She stated:

> If you are good nun, the Buddha, the bodhisattva will provide for us. Like in Christianity you know, this providence. I really believe in providence since I have been ordained. Because I started with zero... this whole place, zero. But whatever I started, people see I am making something, then money will come in... it's just amazing. And really I'm very confident to believe... just be a good nun. Just be a good nun and you will be provided [for].
>
> (Dhammananda 2015)

Ven. Dhammananda (2015) further explained,

> it is difficult unless people trust you... one success in my life, that whatever I do, I always finish, I always succeed. Ever since I was a professor. If I requested a grant to finish this book, I finish this book in time... People trust, so it is just opposite when you come out of academia... in the world of professors you have to write a project proposal and [it] must be very impressive so that they would offer the grant. The grant may come one year after the proposal. If the money doesn't come, you cannot launch this project. But when working as a bhikkhuni it's the opposite... just go ahead and launch the project and the money will come. The money comes because people say 'oh what are you doing? Can we help?'... I really believe that the Buddhas and the bodhisattvas are really seeing our need... I feel very blessed.
>
> (Dhammananda, 2015)

Shirley told of how she was studying up on the 13 Arahat Theris so that she would be able to describe them in more detail to the visitors that she showed around the Monastery. She felt moved by their stories and also felt inspired by the female role models she found in Ven. Dhammananda and the 13 Theris.

> ... with the chanting, the evening chanting, there is one... chant... it's all about them. So it's like, whenever I chant I feel very, like very emotional... we're actually chanting to them... Especially living human being like Dhammananda always like... I really admire her for the things that she do... So it's like... it's very important that we get someone to lead us. But those thirteen Theris are... also good cause it actually inspires you that we should follow Buddha's way and be like them you know? That's why they are up there. If, they say, that if woman do good, nobody actually

> remember, so [Dhammananda] wrote a book on them... so it's like I think you should, you should be able to feel how I feel, yeah?
>
> (Shirley 2015)

Ven. Dhammananda (2015) built the Vihara in stages with the assistance of one of the nuns who has a BA in construction, who was her 'foreman'. They hired specialist contractors who offered their services at a discounted rate. Ven. Dhammananda also recently built a new three-story guest residence where each room has its own ensuite. Again, this was largely a practical consideration as she thought that people were more likely to keep private bathrooms clean and that the guests would feel safer and not have to brave the cold and damp than if they had to walk to shared bathrooms at night or in the early morning (Dhammananda, 2015). Ven. Dhammananda (2015) explained how these facilities are primarily to empower bhikkhunis and nuns to deepen their study at SDKM and that this is her primary social 'outreach', development activity.

> ... this vassa begins at the end of July. We gave sponsorship, scholarship to ten Indian women, nuns and Indian women to come and be trained here as bhikkhunis... Four nuns are coming from Nagpur and maybe two nuns from the southern part of India at least... Because Indian bhikkhunis, even if they were ordained before me, they didn't receive training... So when I met them in Vaishali [at the 2013 Sakydhita conference]... we met, and they asked if I could come and train them. So we went, Theravada bhikkhunis from Vietnam, myself, three bhikkhunis from Thailand, went to train them for one month. And now they [are coming] here... among four of them, one of them speaks good English, so she will be translating for the three and my idea is we will sit down and work together; I teach them in English, she translate for them. And they write their own bhikkhunis' handbook in their own language... so that's my little contribution that I could do to help the Buddha return Buddhism to India, return the bhikkhunis to India soil.
>
> (Dhammananda 2015)

Another sacred place in the Monastery complex is the Medicine Buddha Temple at the rear of the property for healing meditation, which was inspired by a vision Ven. Dhammananda had seven years before she was ordained. It contains a large blue Buddha statue, similar to a Medicine Buddha in the Tibetan tradition, although Ven. Dhammananda had not seen such a Buddha before he appeared to her. The statue was cast in metal in a wax mould in a traditional Thai style, although according to Ven. Dhammananda, Thai people are not so familiar with this type of Medicine Buddha. She also recounted how a Tibetan Rinpoche had conducted a 'breaking the ground ceremony' on the site that would later house the Temple, and how the bhikkhunis returned on the eighth day and fifteenth day of the waxing and waning moon to chant and pray for sufficient funds to complete the project which eventually came to them

(Dhammananda 2015). Ven. Dhammananda (2015) lists it as the third most sacred space in the Monastery.

> ... that space; that is for the medicine Buddha, that's for healing... and he is particularly very beautiful at night because when we turn on the light, the light comes from behind and it's blue... That is his radiance... He radiates in... blue colour... So each [place] has different meaning. If you want to do healing, for healing purpose we would go there.
>
> (Dhammananda 2015)

For Shirley, the Medicine Buddha Temple was a very special place, although as it was at the back of the complex and quite far away from the other buildings she would only go there for weekend teachings or with a companion. She described the feeling of meditating there as 'fantastic... the feeling is very nice. And very soothing, you can hear birds... the feeling is very nice, very, very nice... it's very peaceful inside there, very, very peaceful' (Shirley 2015). When asked why it feels so nice and peaceful, Shirley (2015) replied,

> to me, I think it's... it's the energy when you pray. When you go inside and pray... When you pray to any statue of Buddha, of any goddess, the energy will be there... every day [the] energy will be there. And then you can feel it...
>
> (Shirley 2015)

Shirley (2015) recounted a story of the Medicine Buddha's healing abilities, despite her initial doubts:

> At first I don't believe... when I first came... you can actually ask for curing of any illness in your family member... so what happened was my uncle was in hospital so I just did talk to Buddha please heal him, let him be well, let him have a long life, and he was like cured fully you know, so I say thank you to Buddha, I say thank you to Buddha that day...
>
> (Shirley 2015)

She also spoke of the importance of having faith, similar to that displayed by one of the Arahat Theris, and confidence in the Buddha to answer your prayers.

> ... when we are a Buddhist and we pray so it's like we have confidence when we pray... exactly like when you pray to Jesus Christ, Mother Mary, exactly the same. You talk to them every day, every day; you have strong confidence that God will be there to help when you need them. Even though it doesn't happen today, tomorrow but you know he's there to help you... I talk to Buddha every day and give me more confidence, give me more energy... and I think I have it... especially wisdom, I need wisdom you know? [laughs] It's like, you must have faith in whatever you are

> praying to... I think that's important, faith... if you don't believe in what you're doing, then I don't think you should be doing it right?
>
> (Shirley 2015)

While the Medicine Buddha Temple was very sacred to Shirley, both Ven. Dhammavanna and Shirley said the library, where their Dhamma classes were conducted, was their favourite place. The library was built by Ven. Dhammananda later than the original Monastery buildings but before the Yasodhara Vihara and new residences (Dhammananda 2015).

> My favourite space oh [laugh], normally I stay in the bookstore, but oh I love to stay in the library... [the] windows like this [louvers] old style... it is peaceful and windy... in the corner... you can see the garden... the stone that you can walk [on]... the Dhammananda do it herself... with her disciple. I can feel peaceful there... when I sit there, and I go to study the Tripitaka... or to anything. I feel, oh thank you... Dhammananda... that I can have the place that we can share with the people.
>
> (Dhammavanna 2015)

Shirley (2015) also said that the library was her favourite place and that she spent most of her days here when she wasn't assisting guests or working in the gardens and grounds. The Bodhi tree garden was described as one of the Monastery's most sacred sites. The first Bodhi tree, planted by Voramai, grew from a seed from Bodhgaya, India, related to the Bodhi tree that Buddha sat under when he was enlightened. The tree that stands at SDKM today is from a sapling of Voramai's original Bodhi tree and Ven. Dhammananda (2015) described it as important given its connection to India and as 'it is a sign of enlightenment'. Ven. Dhammavanna (2015) also described it as 'the sign of the Buddha'.

Ven. Dhammananda planted the surrounding bamboo and frangipani garden, as she believes a natural setting is conducive to good practice. She has also been planting more large trees for practical reasons around the property as they provide much needed shade (Dhammananda 2015). Ven. Dhammananda (2007, p. 8) recounted how when Maha Pajapati asked Buddha for advice on how to practice as a bhikkhuni he told her that both Sanghas should 'follow dhamma to be separated (from society)' and 'to follow dhamma which leads to quietude'. In one of her earlier books, she explained how the Buddha lived much of his life 'close to nature' and instructed his followers to have deep respect for all life, as witnessed in the first precept 'not to kill' (Kabilsingh 1998, p. 2). She also said that the contemporary ecological crisis is a result of 'so-called development', which has focused too much on physical and material needs. Instead, she stated that 'a happy society must also be developed both physically and spiritually' (Kabilsingh 1998, p. 3).

In the Bodhi tree garden there is also a small shrine that Shirley (2015) explained was dedicated to what she called 'garden angels' that protected the Monastery.

> in the [Malay] Chinese belief, I think here also… I'm not sure… when you go into temple, you have to pay respect to whatever God we are praying. And when you go into the home, we have to also pay respect to the people at home… So it's like when you are here you also have to make sure that we pay respects… when I first came here, it's like I tell her my name and… I'm here to do merit and whatever good things I do I would also like to share with you and… please protect me and give me have a peaceful night… it's like it's a way of respect, even for the, I call garden angel because in Malaysia we call garden angels, I don't know what they call here… is exactly the same to them also… It's the only way to pay respect to them so they don't harm us, or give us any scary nights.
>
> (Shirley 2015)

The SDKM community is committed to sustainable practices of recycling and organic gardening. They generate compost from food waste that provides good soil for the gardens. They also grow seeds that are GMO free, linked to the Thai Royal seed project (Dhammananda, 2015). Ven. Dhammananda (2015) said that these practices are not only for her community's benefit but that they also wish to inspire their visitors, so they 'set a kind of example that to grow your own vegetables is easy' and that you can do this in an urban setting where space is somewhat scarce. They also have a visiting doctor who has a free clinic at the Monastery on Sundays focused on holistic health care for the nuns and people in the surrounding neighbourhood.

Ven. Dhammananda (2015) follows, and encourages her pupils to follow, the Buddha's and the Bodhisattva's way of life, which is not only focusing on personal enlightenment but also on helping others. She believes in the importance of community/Sangha and of equanimity, which are central to the Buddha's teachings.

> Here we emphasise the bodhisattva's precept, path, because the Buddha walked this path before he became the Buddha. And if we want to follow his teaching, we should also follow the path that he had taken long, long before he was born as Prince Siddhartha to be enlightened as the Buddha. So I emphasise that. So some people will say 'this is my work, I finish my work and that's fine' I go scot-free… [but I say] 'no this sister has not finished work, you go and help her'… so it's very much dependent kind of understanding that we should be helping each other.
>
> (Dhammananda, 2015)

The nuns' daily work hours play a significant role in fostering this communal awareness.

> I think that is how we make, we create community, community based awareness, very important. And working together is an equaliser, I call it 'an hour of equaliser', because we come to the temple like this, education

> wise, upbringing wise, is all different, this is the only time that they come to work together. Same thing. It doesn't matter if you have only two grades of education I just need your two hands, come. Or, if you come with a PhD or a Master's degree, that's fine I don't need that, you come with your two hands. That's how we work together.
>
> (Dhammananda 2015)

Shirley (2015) also spoke of the importance of helping one another and working together as a community.

> It is a community work and I think Dhammananda want us to be, want us to group together so that there's a team working spirit together…so when job is assigned for the day, it's like naturally, everybody will know what to do. If you work well in that job, when you start doing everybody will start to help in with whatever things that we can do. Like you, you take a broom and sweep off all the grass from the ground right, so everybody will just chip in, like, follow the leader. Monkey see, monkey do! [Laugh] That's what we do here.
>
> (Shirley 2015)

Shared rituals and experiences, including those which sacralise space, are also important in creating an interdependent community awareness.

> You see a mound here… a dog passed away just before you came… all of us help dig the ground, bury her and did the blessing together. Some of the nuns cried; they never thought we would give much importance to the death of a dog. I said the dog was our member, this dog was our member so we treat her as much as how we would have treated each one of us… we make blessing, we light candles, we light incense to say goodbye to her, we bring flowers to her… I didn't realise that it was a great teaching… that was the first time for all of them coming as a community to witness, to say goodbye to one member of us, so… The teaching comes like this. And it was impressive for them because they never had witnessed before like this.
>
> (Dhammananda 2015)

The weekly alms round conducted in the surrounding streets, and the nuns' community outreach to a juvenile detention centre for boys and a women's prison were also noteworthy development activities conducted by the bhikkhunis at SDKM.

After an evening chanting session one night, Ven. Dhammananda, two senior bhikkhuni and one attendant recounted a recent visit to a juvenile detention centre for young men near the Monastery. Ven. Dhammananda explained that she chose two senior nuns for this outreach initiative so that the young men would see them as grandmothers or aunties. She asked the team to report back to the nuns about their experience at the detention centre.

The nuns gave a moving account of how they were welcomed by the senior staff, and how the vast majority of young men displayed a respectful attitude toward them. The nuns handed out slips of paper with a prayer for forgiveness written on them. They explained how everyone had made mistakes in their lives, and over lifetimes, and that mistakes were common. They also reassured the boys that as they were young perhaps they had made relatively few mistakes.

One of the older boys was chosen to lead them all in saying this prayer. The nuns were told by the staff that he had actually killed two people. He was covered in tattoos, on his neck and face that elongated his eyes, and while at first he appeared quite frightening the nuns said that they could tell that he was a good person. They described how the boys had greeted them with hands in prayer position and bows and chants of 'Sadhu, Sadhu, Sadhu'. One of the nuns described how she thought that about 60 per cent of the boys really took the forgiveness prayer seriously. After the prayer the nuns handed out white blessing strings, which the young men accepted, some even asked for a second one in case the first one broke.

Afterwards one of the boys sang a moving song about the power of the heart and once again, the nuns recounted that they really felt that these boys, with the right opportunities could lead better lives and be better people. As they were leaving one of the nuns wanted to turn around but could not as she was afraid she might cry, and that would not be appropriate for a nun. She wiped away tears as she told her story to her community who listened carefully, with their hands in prayer position.

These boys will visit SDKM in two weeks' time for a one-day working bee. Their detention centre is poorly funded and the food is very simple, so the nuns will be sure to provide them with the best possible food on the day of their visit. Ven. Dhammananda has promised to return to the boy's centre to speak with the young men individually as she thinks they may benefit from being able to speak with a senior bhikkhuni about their errors. All of the bhikkhuni said that they were really happy to be able to make a difference to these young men's lives.

The nuns also regularly visit a women's provincial prison, where they are warmly welcomed. Some of the inmates even come to the Monastery after they have been released for temporary ordination. Ven. Dhammananda (2015) recounted how when they are freed 'they want to start a new life and they would like to start with ordination. Even for nine days that's fine… and we hope that we'll put them on the right path.'

Conclusion

The bhikkhunis and nuns embody the sacred space of the Monastery, of the Buddha, Dhamma and Sangha, in their robes and with their shaved heads, prayers and blessing strings, and take it with them wherever they go. Whether it is on an alms round, or a visit to the detention centre or prison, they bring the sanctity of the Monastery with them, and sacralise new spaces with not only their prayers and rituals but also their very presence and interaction with other beings. Be it with a bow, or look or smile, there are moments of quiet exchanges that are powerful in transforming ordinary moments into sacred moments. And it is in these moments that development occurs, according to their Buddhist framework, most importantly the development of wisdom and a good heart.

Applying Harvey's (2004) tripartite model of space to the Monastery, the buildings are examples of physical and legal entities situated in absolute space, independent of matter. This absolute space in Buddhist terms is what naturally resides within and around us, and is best contacted and realised through stilling the mind. SDKM provides several sacred places conducive to such practice. It also has created the mental space for such so-called spiritual development to occur, through sacralising rituals and years and years of chanting and prayers that according to the nuns have generated a powerful energy in the Monastery's sacred places, which deepens people's experiences within them.

In terms of relative space, the Monastery is connected to the local neighbourhood, and flows of visitors and residents, as well as natural resources, such as power, food and water, which sustain it. This is a multi-dimensional flow as the bhikkhunis also travel out for development, outreach and advocacy activities, which then creates new networks, real and virtual, and draws new visitors to the Monastery complex. In terms of relational space, it must be considered within broader contexts such as the global Buddhist women's social movement and the current environmental crisis, as well as the Monastery's historical value and the significance it holds in people's personal and collective memories. In this case, we must also consider the SDKM's online presence and larger Buddhist women's online networks as playing a significant role in their development activities. These 'third spaces' enable social action, by drawing upon traditional and modern narratives and technologies, centred on usurping dominant patriarchal narratives within Buddhism and improving women's opportunities for practice and recognition within Buddhism. This activism is also part of the movement's members' spiritual discipline, by following the Bodhisattva's way of life, pledging to help all beings to overcome suffering – in this case caused by gender discrimination – and to reach enlightenment (Tomalin et al. 2015).

While religious places can be constructed to enforce and preserve dominant power structures, they can also be used to challenge them and this is certainly the case at SDKM. Thai Bhikkhunis have acquired and consecrated the land, overseen the building of an Uposatha Hall, residences, a library, a Medicine Buddha Temple and a Yasodhara Vihara. Statues of the thirteen Arahat Theris serve as protectors and guides to the nuns and visitors. Ven. Dhammananda, the Abbess teaches the Dhamma and serves as a role model of a living female Bodhisattva, serving others and liberating them from suffering. A Bodhi tree, a symbol of the Buddha's enlightenment occupies a central place in the Monastery, where respect for nature is encouraged through organic gardening and holistic health care.

The temples, statues, gardens and website of SDKM have all been planned and constructed to allow for its residents and visitors to tap into this at once absolute and basic nature of space, within and around themselves, by creating peaceful sites, conducive to meditation, healing, practice and higher learning. The sacred places within the Monastery have been designed to inspire, empower and support the bhikkhunis by highlighting the significance of the life stories of both historical and contemporary women in Buddhism, the thirteen Arahat Theris, Bhikkhuni Ta Tao and Ven. Dhammananda in particular. Living or remembered they serve as embodied role models and reminders of women's capacity to reach enlightenment and to carry out development activities, to help others to be free from suffering and to reach enlightenment also. These are Buddhist ideals, and can be found in the Buddha's, Ven. Ta Tao's and Ven. Dhammananda's teachings. The places within SDKM, including its online presence, bring them to life in relative and relational space, interconnected with the local area and the broader Buddhist women's social movement globally.

Notes

1 There are many variations in the spellings of Buddhist terms. In this chapter we have used the spelling, acronyms and titles provided on the Songdhammakalyani Monastery (SDKM)/ThaiBhikkunis website's English version.
2 Ven. Dhammananda was interviewed for this case study and allowed her comments to be identified in this chapter. They are cited as (Dhammananda 2015), as the interview was conducted in 2015.
3 Ven. Dhammavanna was interviewed for this case study and allowed her comments to be identified in this chapter. They are cited as (Dhammavanna 2015), as the interview was conducted in 2015.
4 Shirley was interviewed for this case study and allowed her comments to be identified in this chapter. They are cited as (Shirley 2015), as the interview was conducted in 2015.

References

Alliance for Bhikkunis n.d., Home, viewed on 7 July 2015, http://www.bhikkhuni.net.

Dhammananda, B. (Kabilsingh, C.) 2007, *Beyond gender*, Foundation for Women, Law and Rural Development and Women's Studies Centre, Faculty of Social Sciences, Chiang Mai University, Chiang Mai.

Dhammananda, B. (Kabilsingh, C.) 2012, *Herstory*, Thai Tibet Centre, Bangkok.

Dhammananda, B. (Kabilsingh, C.) 2014, 'Bhikkhuni Ta Tao: Paving the way for future generations', in K.L. Tsomo (ed.) *Eminent Buddhist women*, State University of New York Press, New York, pp. 61–70.

Fenn, M.L. & Koppedrayer, K. 2008, 'Sakyadhita: A transnational gathering place for Buddhist women', *Journal of Global Buddhism*, vol. 9, pp. 45–48.

Gross, R.M. 1993, *Buddhism after patriarchy: A feminist history, analysis, and reconstruction of Buddhism*, State University of New York Press, Albany.

Harvey, D. 2004, 'Space as a key word', paper for Marx and Philosophy Conference, 29 May 2004, Institute of Education, London.

Kabilsingh, C. 1998, *Buddhism and nature conservation*, Thai Tibet Centre, Phra Nakorn.

Kustiani, 2013, 'Examining the date of Mahāpajāpatī's Ordination', in K.L. Tsomo (ed.), *Buddhism at the grassroots, 13th Sakyadhita international conference on*

Buddhist women, Sakyadhita International Association of Buddhist Women, New Delhi, pp. 124–127.

Owen, L.B. 1998, 'On gendered discourse and the maintenance of boundaries: A feminist analysis of the *bhikkhuni* order in Indian Buddhism', *Asian Journal of Women's Studies*, vol. 4, no. 3, pp. 8-60.

Sakyadhita n.d., *Home*, viewed on 7 July 2015, http://www.sakyadhita.org.

Songdhammakalyani Monastery n.d. *Home*, viewed on 7 July 2015, http://www.thaibhikkhunis.org/eng2014/contact.html.

Tomalin, E., Starkey, C. & Halafoff, A. 2015 'Cyber sisters: Buddhist women's online activism and practice', in D. Enstedt, G. Larrson & E. Pace (eds.), *Religion and internet*, Annual Review of the Sociology of Religion Series vol. 6, Brill, Leiden and Boston, pp. 11–33.

Tsomo, K.L. 2009, *Buddhist women in a global multicultural community*, Sukhi Hotu Press, Kuala Lumpur.

Yogini Project n.d. Home, viewed on 7 July 2015, http://theyoginiproject.org.

5 Kalani, 'nature, culture, wellness' and sustainable development

... when I got here... I didn't have this greenhouse or any real facilities at all. So I had to... start to form the heart of what we have here [now]... we began taking down... some of the invasive trees, and feeding those to our bananas, and we planted some extra banana clumps all around, and we covered an old [section] of debris... with pumpkins... Applying a little permaculture there, the pumpkins to keep the weeds down and to produce some food for us. And then we began expanding the garden beds here, and creating more of those... we created the nursery and what we call the clubhouse, this is our work space in here where we mix soil, pot plants, have other tools stored and everything...

... this worm bin was already here, so we got that moving along better, and the worm bin is actually what I call a soil generator, because there's all sorts of stuff living in there that breaks down the material that we put in there. And mostly what we put in there is weedy material... the liliko'i vines, when I prune those, those will go in there and then we get all sorts of different bugs. And they all break it down. There're lizards in there, there's centipedes in there, there's occasional [laugh] rodents in there, spiders, everything in there. And then all that stuff breaks stuff down, and then the worms come along and eat all that and break it down further, and that makes really fantastic fertiliser, the world's best fertiliser...

When we look at this space, this was a really nice crew building period in our time here, because we were able to work together to design a really functional space and everybody felt a little ownership in it, and I think that's really important...

... let's go on in, wander in the nursery... so we've got some decorative plants, some native plants, some medicinal plants and a lot of food plants. Like here we have papaya trees, these are strawberries... I have a teak seedling right here, a little baby teak, these are nitrogen fixing trees called scrambled egg trees that'll be incorporated into the landscape as decorative, but they'll also have the function of feeding the landscape. I have some variegated ginger here, which is a decorative variety that's really beautiful. Some cherimoya, Jamaican liliko'i, a basil down here, I have cashews, begonias, gamboge. I have some native Hawaiian hibiscus. This is māmaki, it's a Hawaiian medicinal. This is a medicinal sort of oregano, you can smell that one... It's really potent... And this is another fun one... this one's chocolate mint... Yeah [laugh][inhales]... I really like that one [laugh]... these are coral trees, another nitrogen-fixing tree. Mountain apple, this is a canoe plant that makes nice fruit. And this side, on the left we've got a bunch of our vegetable plants that go in our vegetable gardens, eggplants, peppers, oh I've got giant liliko'i babies over here! It makes a liliko'i, a passionfruit that's the size of an adult human head... It's huge.

Pineapples, we're cloning some cranberry hibiscus right here, we've got ice-cream bean, peach palms... rollinia, abiu, kalanchoe the 'leaf of life'. Tulsi basil, smell that one, break that one up a little bit... that's one of my favorites... patchouli, eggfruit, mamey sapote, jackfruit, tamarillo, fig... lemon balm... jabuticaba... mysore raspberry... cardamom, asparagus, some native Hawaiian trees, this one's called 'ākia and then this one is called 'ohe makai, we have a bunch of surinam cherries, there's probably 50 surinam cherries here, 50 soursop trees, a bunch of rollinias...

... this is a future forest, this is the future food source for this entire property. And so this is all stuff we've put together since I've been here... As you see on the outside of the building, also... we're trying to catch as much water as we can up here, 'cause water of course is a major resource, and if we can catch our own then we save a lot of energy and don't have to use the water that's stored away in the aquifer where we'd bring water from the pump.

So, here [in the garden] we have some 'olena, which is turmeric, this is a canoe plant that they brought here, its used around the world medicinally and in a lot of food... we've inter-planted with milkweed to attract butterflies, and also to keep other weeds out... Over here, we've got basil and eggplants and zinnias and sunflowers and fennel and more milkweed in here. Jicama flowers and jicama plants over there. [There's a] carpenter bee! Yeah look at them all up there, just working it! And then a dragonfly going by... that's one of the most amazing things about this space to me is that there's so much life when you just slow down and you look at all the insects that are cruising around, and all the bugs that are cruising around. It's a place that you wouldn't realise is just filled with life and you just take a moment and it's just utterly packed with it...

... what we're trying to do is tap into the most sustainable system we can, because we're in a place to make a model... permaculture, I do believe once you get it up and running can take care of all your needs. That's what it's really all about, taking care of all your shelter needs, all your food needs and your fuel needs, your energy needs. It just takes a while actually to get it going. And by a while I mean, you just can't get it going in four months, like you could with conventional agriculture. You could come in here with bulldozers and till the soil and inject a bunch of chemicals and then grow a really fast crop of genetically modified stuff or you can put in a system that nourishes itself through time and then gets richer and richer and more abundant through time. And it just takes a little bit more time, more patience, and that's what we're doing here... so, around us right now is what I consider the living seed bank... that's a long term investment.

(Laaback[1] 2015)

Introduction

Kalani is one of the world's oldest retreat centres. It is located in Pāhoa in Puna, one of the nine districts of Hawai'i, the Big Island. Puna is blessed with natural wonders including lava flows, black sand beaches, geothermal tidal pools and native mahogany forests. It is an economically poor area, compared with the rest of Hawai'i, and the fastest growing district on the Big Island. Puna's economy centers on agriculture and tourism, and Kalani is among its main attractions.

Kalani has long offered an opportunity for people to escape the fast pace of city life and to spend time in nature, in community, and to participate in educational programmes for their personal growth and wellbeing. More recently Kalani has become increasingly focused on issues of sustainability and its Permaculture Program, now in its second year, is at the centre of Kalani's commitment to model ecologically sustainable development. The programme's Manager, Scott Laaback and his team are creating new sacred places at Kalani, teeming with life and inspiration, as he described above. The land on which Kalani was first built has long been sacred to the Hawaiian people and contains many sacred places including a temple (heiau) and school (halau) site, as well as an old agricultural field system and family burial grounds. The founders of Kalani, Richard Koob and Earnest Morgan, first 'ascended in love' with the Big Island's natural beauty 40 years ago (Koob, personal communication, 9 February 2016). They fulfilled their dream of creating a retreat centre in Hawai'i, with deep reverence for the land, its people, their traditions and its sacred places, a reverence that they have passed on to new generations of Kalani staff and volunteers.

An ethic of care and respect – for oneself, for one another, for the earth – along with a deep awareness of the interconnectedness of all life and the importance of community, are embodied in Kalani's spaces, activities, and in its leadership. Kalani is a community of 150 staff and volunteers, most of whom live on or at least nearby the 120 acre property. They can accommodate up to 150 guests and have 24,000 square feet of workshop space for retreats run by world-class facilitators and weekly classes for the Kalani and local Puna community.

The Kalani Puna Community Arts & Classes flyer describes the centre as 'Presenting NATURE, CULTURE, and WELLNESS within sustainable, educational programs that honor Hawaii's native and diverse heritage'. The classes include many styles of yoga and dance, with Ecstatic Dance and Hula among the highlights, and ukulele, lauhala weaving, lei making, meditation, writing, life drawing, life skills, capoeira, volleyball, fierce volleyball, an Open Mic night, nature tours and trips to local markets. Many of the classes are offered for free or on a donation basis, enabling greater participation by the Puna community.

The studio spaces have screen walls and windows that keep insects and wildlife out but which let plenty of light and air in. They also look out onto forests and tropical gardens and the sounds of birds and frogs permeate the spaces while people are doing yoga, or dancing, or making leis. The varied levels of accommodation, from private modern cottages, to private rooms in the original buildings, to shared dormitories, to large tents, also have screens for windows, and are situated in beautiful natural settings. The Dining Lanai is completely open-planned with no walls, and with long wooden tables, where delicious meals are served and stimulating conversations are held. Kalani's commitment to acceptance of diversity is expressed here in the many food choices that are offered with no sense of judgement. People can freely chose vegan and gluten free, vegetarian, seafood or meat options. Food is abundantly offered, while waste is discouraged and recycled. Kalani also has a large swimming pool, two hot tubs and sauna where clothing is optional. Massage and other wellness treatments, including a Watsu pool with healing properties, are available in the healing centre that is also surrounded by ponds and lush gardens. A large reclining statue of Buddha is visible from the pool, gently reminding community members of the importance and sanctity of repose.

The Hawaiian sacred places, while mentioned on Kalani's website, are not shown on Kalani's maps nor are they advertised to visitors. On occasions ceremonies are conducted at the heiau temple site, and open to the Kalani and wider community but otherwise visitors may simply stumble across the heiau and halau school sites when exploring the community. They are not off limits, but they are somewhat hidden. Visitors can also see the large old coconut and mango fruit trees around the property and the giant monkeypod tree near the camping grounds, which is deemed sacred by some community members. The burial site remains completely unmarked and unexplored out of respect to the local community.

The pathway to the heiau site leads off from the main EMAX Workshop space car park, near the entry to the Kalani property. The site is covered in sacred native lama trees, laua'e ferns, coconut and pandanas palms. The stone foundations of the heiau platform have been rebuilt and a small sign that says 'QUIET PLEASE MEDITATION AREA' marks the site.

The school site is not far from the heiau on the other side of Kalani's driveway. A small laminated sign on the path explains the significance of the site to visitors. It reads:

> KAMA'ILI HALAU
>
> Heritage School Site
>
> This coastal area, bordered by stone walls, is the site of the ancient Hawaiian Kama'ili School. Kini Pe'a, a native of this Puna district and a Kalani Honua founding board member, stated that the school structure is believed to exist until 1990, when his mother was the last teacher. Prior to missionary influences, the school likely was devoted to Hawaiian culture. Please honor this site with respectful meditation, and stay on the path, lush with laua'e fern and shaded by Kamani (mahogony).
>
> Mahalo

Another sacred place nearby, across the red road from the halau site and the entrance to Kalani is The Point. Through the ancient native orange Kamani forest, under a coconut palm there is a wooden bench on a cliff face overlooking the ocean. It is here at The Point where Richard and Earnest's visions of Kalani first began to be realised.

Kalani's beginnings

Kalani's co-founder and Director Emeritus, Richard Koob[2] (2015), explained that Kalani means 'heaven' and that its full name 'Kalani Honua', means 'heaven on earth... it's really a combination of the physical and spiritual'. Richard grew up on a farm in a small village in the south west of Minnesota and has always felt 'very connected with nature'. He was born and raised in an artistic and sporty Catholic family of eight, and described how founding Kalani was in ways 'really like a recreation of what I grew up with in the village, but in a more open and diverse, and progressive way' (Koob 2015).

As a young man, Richard studied German literature at Freiburg University and it was then that he 'began to break away from the restrictive Catholic veil' of his upbringing (Koob 2014, p. 3). His time in Europe shaped his views on, and resistance to, the Vietnam War and also led him to spend three months in Cuba on the first Brigada Venceremos with Students for a Democratic Society. He became involved in radical politics in New York City and operated an underground press, which printed flyers for the Black Panthers, the Young Lords and others, in a basement south of Houston. He was also very much involved in the beginning of the gay rights, LGBT movement in the USA in the 1960s (Koob 2014, 2015).

Richard met his lifelong partner, and co-founder of Kalani, Earnest Morgan, when he was handing out flyers on Christopher Street, Greenwich Village, for a one year anniversary event to commemorate the 1969 Stonewall uprising. Richard recounted how he was immediately enamoured with Earnest, who was a professional ballet dancer that had grown up in rural O'ahu, Hawai'i (Koob 2014, 2015).

Early on in their relationship, Earnest and Richard saw an advertisement posted by a well-known choreographer who was looking for athletic people with no formal dance training to join their company. Richard got the job and began performing all over New York City (Koob 2015). He spoke of how much and why he enjoyed it.

> I loved it... it involved audiences, it was very communal. In a way, it was like a mini Kalani... in terms of how it was just about outreach and bringing people in and changing their lives.
>
> (Koob 2015)

The educational and transformative aspects of dance, combined with a love of nature, and affinity for Hawai'i, led Earnest and Richard to eventually create Kalani. From New York, they travelled to Paris, where Earnest danced with Jacques Garnier's premier modern dance company Théâtre du Silence, and Richard worked with Sheela Raj, in her company Le Cercle. Raj, who was originally from India, had danced with Twlya Tharp in New York and was trained in yoga as well as modern ballet. Spending time in her company, which embodied 'circle culture', was 'very transformative' for Richard and Earnest (Koob 2014, 2015).

They toured extensively around Europe and Russia, finally settling in Provence, in preparation for the Avignon dance festival. Richard expressed his love of Southern France and the beginnings of their vision stirring here:

> In many ways our dream was well represented here. There would be no more hustle and bustle of New York City or Paris for us. We couldn't imagine another city we'd want to live in, should there be one that didn't suck life more than sustain it. We wanted to create our own way, somehow more simply, more wholesome, in nature.
>
> (Koob 2014, p. 3)

Here they contemplated purchasing a disused monastery, on a 'fallow' but previously sacred site, that they could 'reinvent' to set up a centre 'appreciative of diversity', for 'yoga and dance and arts and music; nature, culture and wellness'. It was then that Earnest suggested 'let's go to Hawai'i and do it' as he was wanting to return to his homeland and also on a more practical level he thought that it would be easier to deal with the Hawaiian than the French government given potential language barriers (Koob 2015). At that time, neither of them had heard of Findhorn or other early intentional alternative communities and Richard explained how,

> the anxious world was again screaming its need for places of refuge. We wanted to touch and heal people with something we had found deep within our selves and our experience. So we were drawn to one of the most beautiful and isolated coasts on the most remote islands of the world.
>
> (Koob 2014, p. 4)

Richard exclaimed that 'we came [to Hawai'i] with the intention of starting a retreat center, but we didn't have any idea where!' (Koob 2015). They first settled in Maui, then O'ahu, where Earnest danced with the Honolulu City Ballet and established his own Dance O Hawai'i modern company. Richard apprenticed with the Ballet, danced with the modern Akiko Company, and completed a Master of Fine Arts in Dance at the University of Hawai'i. In Maui they became very close with a 'wonderful musician' Bill Biglow and other artists. Soon they were performing and teaching dance across the islands in many schools and community centres. Both Earnest and Richard were employed as Arts Coordinators for the State Foundation on Culture and Arts, which at the time saw the Big Island 'as being the next growth area'. That is how they came to Hilo in 1975, where they founded the Big Island Dance Council, and first heard about the land for sale that was to become Kalani (Koob 2014, 2015).

Hilo, the second largest city in Hawai'i, had a University of Hawai'i campus. Earnest and Richard studied with 'the great treasure of hula' Auntie Edith Kanaka'ole, and found out that Auntie Edith's sister owned a property in Puna that was for sale (Koob 2015). Richard recalled how,

> we met her, and she was really pleased that we had the intention of having it be non-profit, educational, environmentally focused. And we also found out at that time that it was the site of an ancient Hawai'ian school, which she told us about. And we [also] met in the community here, Kini Pe'a, a native Hawaiian elder, who was President of the Kalapana Community Organization and his mother was the last schoolteacher here in 1900.
>
> (Koob 2015)

Richard said that initially 'it was total jungle' and he recounted how around American Thanksgiving he and Earnest had a picnic at The Point, on the edge of the property overlooking the ocean, where they felt the potential of what they were about to create just as they were about to sign the land sale documents (Koob 2015).

> The Point was just where all the elements came together and just down the way was the lava flowing into the ocean. So, the power of the water, the air, the land... and the 'āina, which is the [Hawaiian] word for the land, literally means 'that which nurtures us' and then Pele [the volcano goddess] and the volcano and the fire, and... you could just feel the mana, the energy. Because we knew it was the school site and we'd dream about what could happen...
>
> (Koob 2015)

The Point remains one of Kalani's most sacred places. At the time Richard said the Puna area was largely populated by indigenous Hawaiians but was in the process of being subdivided and sold off 'sight unseen on TV in Japan and America', following a 'typical pattern of American colonialism'. Yet what they were establishing at Kalani was quite different, given the deep connection and appreciation they had and were further developing with the Hawaiian land, people, life and culture (Koob 2015).

Richard explained how they spent five years connecting with the local community and that the fact that Earnest was originally from Hawai'i helped them to do so. Richard said that while Earnest was African American, and not indigenous Hawaiian,

> he grew up here, [was] born and raised here, and among the Hawaiians I feel there's this concept, and I felt accepted in that way too, when you've been here a while and embrace the culture and the environment that you become Hawaiian. So that was really touching and beautiful for me to, to be invited and to be included in that way.
>
> (Koob 2015)

They 'were made to feel at home by the mana [sacred force] of the area, the aloha [love/heartfelt sincerity] of its residents, and particularly the Kalapana Community Organization leaders', who Richard described as 'the pohaku, the stabilizing foundation rock' of Kalani (Koob 2014, pp. 8–9).

They initially purchased 19 acres of land, with their families' support and loans, and began building Kalani with help from friends and relatives, who were particularly keen to escape the extremely cold conditions of mainland USA in the winter months and head to the warmth of Hawai'i (Koob 2015). Earnest, Richard and Bill built the first cottage on Kalani together, with three poles in the centre representing their relationship. Richard explained how:

> I think that's an example, I feel that, [of] how working together, and working with community and working with the land and the heritage of the land and the spirit of the land, we manifested this new revitalisation of what was here before, because I really feel that the spirits are here and they're strong and we're just tapping into that and they're tapping into us. ... you've heard about the 'aumakua probably? The guiding spirits. Hawaiian families traditionally have an 'aumakua guiding spirit for their family group.
>
> (Koob 2015)

As they acquired more land, and were building extra accommodation and dance and yoga spaces on the property they undertook archeological surveys. During this process they discovered that in addition to the halau Kama'ili School site there was a heiau, a Hawaiian temple site 'to Lono, the God of agricultural abundance', and a traditional 'family cemetery for the Kanaka'ole 'ohana' (Koob 2014, pp. 7–8, 2015). These sites are now protected by the State Historical Registration Program. Further archeological surveys also uncovered an 'old field system', with some remaining fruit trees and stone walls, which the Kalani community also decided to preserve. As the last lava flows in the area were in the 1400s, Richard believed Hawaiians had lived on or near Kalani for at least 500–600 years, if not much longer (Koob 2015).

The District of Puna was one of six autonomous chiefdoms on the island, circa A.D. 1475. The first European contact occurred in 1823, by missionaries who stated that there were 2,000 Hawaiians in the area with an organised 'dryland field system' where taro, sugarcane, sweet potatoes, bananas and bread-fruit were cultivated. A series of epidemics in the 1840s tragically halved the indigenous population, who continued to decline and as a result these early field systems were abandoned and replaced with ranching and commercial growing of coffee and sugarcane (Koob 2014, pp. 14–15). In more recent years the population of Puna has been expanding and there has been a resurgence of interest in Hawaiian culture (DeGenaro 2015).

Richard described how traditionally the land had been divided into ahupua'a, pie-shaped sections belonging to families or 'ohana groups, where 'ohana means 'the circle of all those who breathe together'. This made sure that these 'ohana had access to 'resources of the coast, the ocean as well as the uplands'. At Kalani, they had been able to 'kind of put back together quite a bit of the original ahupua'a' including preserving the 'heiau stone platform site where people can make offerings' and 'the halau or school site and traditional burial grounds' (Koob 2015).

Richard told how, 'with two kahunas, which are Hawaiian spiritual leaders, we re-consecrated the heiau temple site' and 'had ceremonies there'. He also said that, 'with a local hula halau' and with their educational programmes at Kalani, and their outreach programmes in schools and communities around and beyond the Big Island, they have encouraged people to experience and respect Hawai'i's culture, as a foundation for respecting other cultures also (Koob 2015).

In addition to his love of nature and Hawaiian culture, the creative arts and yoga, Richard has also been influenced by Buddhism, and a strong desire to help others to be appreciative and accepting of diversity and therefore of one another. He remembered how at his good friend's child's kindergarten there was a hanging on the wall that included the 'rules for life'. It read: 'Love yourself, respect others, and take care of home, local and global'. He and his friends all agreed 'that's all we really need to know!' (Koob 2015).

Tiki DeGenaro,[3] Kalani's General Manager and Interim Executive Director, commented on the importance of acceptance in Richard and Earnest's lives, and dreams of creating Kalani, which remains central to its mission.

> ... it truly was a vision of the heart and the future, to have a Centre where everyone can come and be accepted, and work on their path, whatever path they chose. And being gay men who had experienced so much bias and prejudice in their lives, they really felt that the heart of Kalani would be a place where everyone was accepted. And everyone could continue on their journey. And it was... like, whatever helps somebody move forward in their life to be loved and accepted and to experience growth through this beautiful nature.
>
> (DeGenaro 2015)

Kalani's vision and development activities

Kalani, now in its fortieth year, comprises 120 acres. They have continued to expand and to host music, dance, yoga, meditation, culinary programmes, and a number of festivals. Yoga and dance are the most popular activities at Kalani, as they have such a large amount of studio space in natural settings, highly conducive to these activities. The Kalani community always encourages its workshop participants to stay on after their course is complete if possible and to explore the surrounding areas of Puna and the Big Island. Most of their visitors and volunteers are from the western United States, due to its proximity, and then Canada and the eastern United States, as people are very keen to escape the cold and long winters in these areas. Kalani also has many visitors from Japan, Europe, Australia and New Zealand (DeGenaro 2015).

Its founders were 'ahead of their time', given the more recent growing global appeal of retreat centres and interest in sustainable living (DeGenaro 2015). Tiki explained that,

> we feel very fortunate here… our doors are open wide… some retreat centers just focus on a certain thing, and we don't… [we] have a hundred different workshops a year and we are open to anything as long as… it makes sense on somebody's path and as long as it doesn't hurt anyone. We've had some pretty unique kinds of subject matters but mostly it's all about self-help.
>
> (DeGenaro 2015)

Tiki, who previously worked in 'the big corporate world' of finance, marketing and management, first heard about Kalani through friends who were conducting workshops on 'the retreat circuit' internationally. She recalled how they used to tell her about 'this funky little place that's in a very remote area of the Big Island called Kalani'. One time they invited their friends to join them and Tiki decided to go. She had lived on Kaua'i previously and knew the islands of O'ahu and Maui very well, but she had never been to Hawai'i, the Big Island. She spent a week at Kalani, attending her friend's workshop and then another touring the island. She was really impressed with Kalani and the whole island's natural beauty. Her most lasting impression was that Kalani was 'a fabulous place for people in transition, to really start a journey of self-reflection' (DeGenaro 2015).

Scott, the Permaculture Manager, recounted how 'a crisis of conscience about what's happening in the world' and 'a conscious recognition' that he 'needed to do something that was… more aligned with what [he] was feeling internally and what [he] was becoming aware' of led him to Kalani (Laaback 2015). He had previously been a wildland firefighter in the American West before quitting his job and moving to Hawai'i.

> I did that for about a decade, and I really loved it but… I started learning some things about the constructs of society and different filters for looking at things, like the filter of matriarchy and patriarchy and I thought to myself, this is human beings enacting kind of a patriarchal view of how things should be, how our interaction with nature should be. And it's saying that we can dominate nature… and unfortunately [laugh] the scary part about that and the outflow of that is we *are* nature; we're doing that to ourselves in that process. And so I really try to align my life with something that's along those lines, more along the lines of moving away from supporting that patriarchal, human against nature [view] and moving toward bringing people closer to nature.
>
> (Laaback 2015)

Scott explained how food was central to his philosophy of sustainable living, given that he had always loved food and cooking and had worked as a chef but even more so as food systems were 'the biggest agents of climate change' (Laaback 2015). He stated that,

> practically what I realised is there has to be a change in the way agriculture is done on this planet and ultimately, what that comes down to is changing the way we perceive the rest of the world. And moving away from seeing it as a resource to be extracted, and rather just part of ourselves to be interacted with in a healthy fashion.
>
> (Laaback 2015)

For Ali Slous[4] (2015), Kalani's Communication Manager, the pace and pressures of modern life led her to seek alternative ways of living, and this led her to Kalani.

> I was working in advertising in New York City for about the past ten plus years, living in a very urban Manhattan environment… And finding yoga… was kind of, the major turning point in my life in terms of deciding I think, just getting more in touch with my inner guidance system, my higher self or however you like to refer to it, and just starting to feel like I needed to change, that the life I had created for myself in New York was no longer serving me on the deepest levels. And so I decided to leave New York, and I was looking for a place to transition and that's how I found Kalani. I typed in yoga, volunteer and Hawai'i and Kalani came right up to the top of my search, and I started as a three-month kitchen volunteer, but I came on a one-way ticket and yeah, and so in… just under two years, I've served as a volunteer in the kitchen and then worked my way up through communications and now I'm managing that team.
>
> (Slous 2015)

Ali further described how,

> I believe we're creating the new earth, I believe that the systems and world as it currently is, I don't think it's serving us as individuals or collectively. I think there are a lot of unhappy people out there, but there are also a lot of sick people out there and I believe that the root of illness has to do with this sense that we're not really living our purpose, that we're not being true to ourselves and we're not taking care of ourselves like on that deep level, and I think that's why yoga has expanded so much is that people have found, ok, getting on a mat, I can have some time for myself, I can breathe, I can just *be*. And so I think the world as it currently is really needs to shift, and some people like myself have just basically just been like 'you know what, I just need to go somewhere else and try a different way'. And so I think of Kalani as one expression of that need for a new, a new way of doing things, new systems, new perspectives… and focusing on the whole individual, that we're not just our job, that we're

> not just what we do, and that we *are* each unique beings that are here for a purpose and to express ourselves fully and to feel good, and to be healthy, and free, and creative and happy.
>
> (Slous 2015)

In addition to providing a space for its guests and visitors to slow down and focus more on nature, culture and wellness, Kalani is very much committed to sharing its facilities with, and providing educational opportunities for, the local Puna community which is 'the most economically disadvantaged area in Hawai'i' (Slous 2015). Ali stated that 'part of our non-profit educational status is because we offer classes and events to the community, often free or by donation… so there's this huge breadth of educational experiences that are available to the community that lives here' (Slous 2015).

According to Tiki, as Puna is a remote area there aren't that many local activities, so as a result, 'Kalani is like a real hub, it's a social place, it's a networking [opportunity for locals], they really appreciate the classes and events we host'. The local community participates in educational activities and events and can also visit Kalani to use the pool or to eat in the Dining Lanai (DeGenaro 2015). In addition to inviting the local community into Kalani, Ali said that 'part of what we're working toward is getting *out* into the community a little bit more'. Her team has organised music and yoga festivals at Kalani, which have included free opening night events and concerts in public parks where 'everyone comes out and brings their… tents and chairs, and there's like families barbequing and it's really beautiful'. She added, 'so that's our offering… to the community to be able to come for classes, workshops and events, meals and, I think that will open up more and more over time', as Puna community members can trade work for a yoga festival pass, for example, or hopefully they may also volunteer in the newer permaculture programme (Slous 2015).

Kalani's sacred places

With regard to Kalani's sacred places, Richard described all of Kalani as sacred, with great reverence for the Hawaiian culture, the halau and heiau sites, the old field systems and 'ohana burial grounds. He also stated that 'even what we're adding to it is sacred' (Koob 2015).

Tiki and Ali also all expressed how they felt that the whole of Kalani, and its surrounding area was a sacred place, with reference to Hawaiian culture and particularly the volcano goddess Pele, the lava, the land and the sea.

> The whole place is sacred… we really feel like the whole thing is definitely scared. Yeah. That we're walking on sacred land. And we're walking on relatively new land… So yeah, people have a reverence. There's so much to learn from nature. And I mean, look outside!… Take lots of big deep breaths here, because the air is *so* clean, the air actually sits on the water,

> on the surface of the ocean for about two weeks until it hits our shores so the water is just *so* magnificent here and yeah I love it [laugh].
>
> (DeGenaro 2015)

> … this whole island is supposed to be a sacred place to the Hawaiians, and… Mauna Kea [volcano] is considered a temple and, I really believe it's *everywhere*, I do, I believe it's us, I believe it's everything… I don't even know how to separate myself. I do believe there are certain sites where maybe the power is more potent, but I do think it's everywhere.… I think there's a literal side to it and a metaphorical side to it… because we are in this place where it's the newest earth on the planet, and I suspect that the lava, because it's this molten earth that's coming out from the core of the earth… I think of it as a mandala in a sense, because it's like *everything*, everything that has ever been is, I don't know, it's hard to put into words, but I think of the lava as this super conductive energy portal, that we have access to by being here. And I imagine that there's some sort of crystalline properties or something where it really *is* channeling energy in a different way. So in that sense I believe that it does have a very powerful, palpable energy here.
>
> (Slous 2015)

> … the Hawaiians believe that Pele [the volcano goddess] is the destroyer, and operator, and creator, and it's very apparent since the island is so new, and lots of land is getting formed every day, there is an active lava flow now… so yeah there's great reverence for Pele, there's great reverence for the land, [the] 'āina… 'that which feeds us'…
>
> (DeGenaro 2015)

Tiki further explained that Pele and the Puna district were associated with healing, which was why yoga and massage, and learning about the healing arts and medicinal plants, such as the noni and mangosteen, was so popular in this area, including at Kalani (DeGenaro 2015).

Scott also said that 'the whole place is a sacred space' because it was both a refuge and a training ground, and that it was important 'to consider the whole place sacred' in order 'to keep the power in it'. Scott discussed the subjectivity of sacredness, stating that 'there are different levels of sacredness, just depending on who views what as sacred' (Laaback 2015).

> 'Sacred' is just what we define our relationship with that place and how that place affects us… E[cstatic] Dance. Some people think it's sacred, like, heavily sacred, I go in there and get that feeling. But somebody else could look at that and just see a bunch of writhing hippies [laugh]. Sweating on each other [laugh]. So that's a definition I think that's human imposed. That being said, it doesn't diminish that relationship that somebody has with that sacred space.
>
> (Laaback 2015)

> I mean, what *is* sacredness? [laugh]… It's really vague. Yeah. 'cause I couldn't even define what's sacred to me except for like nature and all this beauty around here. Like I'm looking here and I'm like this is my temple here, you know?
>
> (Laaback 2015)

Scott explained that unfortunately not everyone had the same kind of reverence for Kalani.

> I see certain things behind the scenes, that people don't necessarily treat the place as sacred, a lot of people come through here and they don't even understand what that even means… it makes me kind of bummed when I see all the trash in the compost… it's kind of amazing how my sacred space is not somebody else's sacred space at all…
>
> (Laaback 2015)

However, he remained optimistic that people could learn to be more respectful and that was part of Kalani's educative mission.

> We are the protectors of this sacred space and one of our functions in that is to educate. And that's the training ground thing. People come through continuously and always will, we're always going to have these problems happening, I'm not trying to be a pessimist, I don't feel pessimistic about it actually, I feel really optimistic that I have this opportunity, and the reason it will never change is because we always have this influx of people, but those people are going to change. And they're going to go out and give that to the rest of the world. And that's huge.
>
> (Laaback 2015)

When asked about the heiau and halau sites, Ali recounted how her team had recently held a special event at the heiau temple and how she has regularly returned there since then.

> … during our New Year's events… I wanted to create a quiet meditation space because I felt like, our New Year's party was different in the sense that… there was no alcohol being served so it was more of a contemplative New Year… there was dancing and revelry and fun, but there was also some more contemplative aspects to it. So we had a fire and a water installation, where you could write something on a piece of rice paper and let it go into the fire. Or you could take a handful of petals, of flowers that were harvested from around the campus, and make a wish and release them into the water. And then the other part of that, outside of the event space was that our horticulture team redid the path to… the heiau… so we had a candle or a torch lit meditation walk there and it was really powerful. And I have noticed that when I've gone back to that site, I've had a moment

> there when I've definitely like… asked for support, or wanted to let something go or reaffirm something to the universe.
>
> (Slous 2015)

Scott reflected on the different waves of people who had lived on Kalani and likened its relationship with sacred places to countries like Turkey or China where 'the current civilisation is built on like ten other civilisation's layers' (Laaback 2015). He explained that,

> part of what we've done is try to preserve certain spaces that could be identified as sacred spaces… And so when I think about the heiau or halau or something, there're a lot of people that don't know that stuff exists on this property. There're a lot of people that don't know what those even are. And there's not a lot of modern activity in those things. It's more of, conceptually we protect those things, and then practically on the ground Trent's [horticulture] crew and my crew go in and do the work to protect those things and sometimes we do some cultural activities around them…
>
> (Laaback 2015)

He also spoke of the importance of preserving Kalani's sacred places and plant life.

> I'm at least trying to respect what was here before in the sense of these archaeological sites, the agricultural fields that are here, and, along the lines of the cultural significance of the plants that are here, the native plants that are still here. I'm trying to do my part in actually preserving that. Because I think, personally I think that is really sacred at this point… The property has many native lama trees, also known as 'Hawaiian ebony', that are sacred to Hawaiians who use it in traditional ceremonies. There are also many native ʻōhiʻa trees that are also considered sacred and connected with Pele. They are an endangered species, as many are dying from a fungal disease. Both species are honored and protected on Kalani.
>
> (Laaback 2015)

Kanali's future

The original 19 acres of Kalani are now owned and run by a non-profit organisation, while the rest of the land is now managed by the non-profit but owned by two Limited Liability Corporations (LLC), which have a Steward Program where members can buy and own cottages on the property, which helps finance Kalani's non-profit activities. The Stewards and their friends and families can stay in the cottages whenever they like and they can also rent them out as a profit-generating activity for themselves and the Kalani community who build and maintain them (Koob 2015; DeGenaro 2015). Tiki explained how this programme is very beneficial for everyone involved as 'we have about 24 stewards so far, and they're people that fall in love with Kalani, love having a place to stay, love being in support of our mission, and also have an opportunity to, make a little revenue and help us out too' (DeGenaro 2015).

Tiki stated how 'you never know what the economy's going to bring' and that this uncertainty provided 'an underlying inspiration for learning how to live on the land, and continuing to grow and take care of your own infrastructure and to create your own housing and to learn how to live together'. She further described how 'they had a great time and people came here and it was considered a haven' but that 'financially it was always very challenging'. Tiki believes that 'to be honest, the internet saved it, because it was pretty much surviving by word of mouth' (DeGenaro 2015). Ali also spoke of the importance of the website and social media more generally in spreading the word about Kalani, attracting new guests and volunteers.

> ... even just anecdotally, in many of my conversations, people have told me they found Kalani through a search... And I believe [the internet has] opened it up tremendously. And the power of social media... because another thing that I'm noticing is that a lot of people are coming because either a friend came here or a family member came here, so there's a really powerful I think word of mouth and social messaging that's being spread right now... so my team also handles our Facebook, YouTube, Instagram, Twitter, and we're thinking of adding Pinterest but we'll see.
>
> (Slous 2015)

Ali added how the social media network not only brought new people to Kalani but also helped globally spread the awareness of alternative ways of being.

> Yeah so [it's a] spider web of getting the word out that there's another way, or that if you really need a break you can just kind of plug yourself in and charge up for a while and then go back out there, and I believe we're creating a really strong ripple effect that way, whether you're here for a week or a month or a year, you're empowering yourself, creating new relationships, and just seeing that life can be just a different way, and then bringing that back out into the world with you.
>
> (Slous 2015)

Ali's team members are also in the process of updating the Kalani website to more accurately reflect the current community (Kalani n.d.; Slous 2015).

In recent years Kalani has faced some additional obstacles with people resisting changes and new growth at times, and in the transitioning of leadership. They are now considering replacing the single Director model with a triumvirate Executive Committee, which may be more appropriate for a community and business, such as Kalani, to better maintain their 'circle culture'. According to Richard, 'three is like a tripod, it's just stronger' and more like a family than a single figurehead (Koob 2015). He also likened it to the trio of Earnest, Bill and himself, who created Kalani's first cottage, and the flows of knowledge in and out of Kalani to a lotus flower,

> in the middle, there's this energy, this trio, of whatever, a directorship kind of energy, and then there's the petals of all the Departments, and services, and there are the bees that are flying in and all the insects that are pollinating, and taking that pollen and energising the world.
>
> (Koob 2015)

Richard explained that what has kept the community strong, and able to cope with these challenges is accepting that 'growing can be good' if done in 'a conscious way'. He also stated 'that we [must always] stand up for what we need to do, to really uphold our vision', which for him is the commitment to further 'educational, nature, culture, wellness', and 'to model sustainable living' (Koob 2015).

The commitment to sustainability is something that they have been focusing on at Kalani more recently, in the past five–ten years particularly. They are growing more of their own food each year, and generating more solar power. They are also looking more towards the Hawaiian field system as a model of sustainable development and self-sufficiency. Kalani held its first two-week permaculture design course in November 2015, as part of a sustainable living skills programme that Scott's Permaculture Department was developing. First they built the permaculture infrastructure, then the gardens and then launched their educational component. Where Kalani needs to import food or building materials they are trying to do so in a more sustainable manner. Their vision is to 'model a thriving planet… for the 8000 or so people that come through every year'. In doing so they are 'connecting with that source', of the original Hawaiian culture, which 'embraces nature'. Richard said, 'I like to keep encouraging that as much as possible' (Koob 2015).

Tiki similarly observed how,

> the way the Hawaiian people were living, was a very sustainable way. They… were really growing their own food, they were living as an extended family, taking care of each other, trying to honor the past traditions… Richard and Earnest fell in *love* with the culture. So they were attempting to learn the language. They learned how to chant, they learned how to hula, and they were certainly learning the 'Hawaiian ways' for how to exist in the jungle. And, so Richard jokes sometimes, that now… it's so *in* and *new* to be sustainable, but really, we're just trying to get back to the way things always were.
>
> (DeGenaro 2015)

Tiki also described the centrality of Hawaiian culture to life at Kalani,

> there's just so much we can learn from the indigenous cultures and… it's… sad that the culture almost got wiped out but now more people speak

> Hawaiian than ever before, and all the traditions are coming back, the weaving, the dancing, the language, the chanting. And we try and, we have so much respect for that, we try and incorporate it into everything we're doing.
> (DeGenaro 2015)

For example, in November 2015, Kalani was honoured to host the Hawai'i Yoga Festival, out of respect for the Hawaiian culture but also as an opportunity to introduce people to it. A Hawaiian elder conducted a chant and blessing ceremony with blessed water and tea leaves to open the festival and the programme included both ancient kahiko and modern 'auana forms of hula. Kalani also hosts weekly Hawaiian hula and cultural classes as part of their regular programme conducted by members of the local community, which are very popular among guests, volunteers and locals (DeGenaro 2015).

While Richard intends to spend more time painting, drawing, playing volleyball, writing, swimming and travelling, to visit other centres 'sharing the culture', he believes his main purpose, as a Kalani founder, is 'to give people a sense of the culture and the Hawaiian language and encourage participation' as he believes this is 'the way to ground yourself here'. Ways in which he encourages connection with 'the life force' include his authoring of the history *Kalani – A Leap of Faith, Hope and Love*, the *E Ho Mai: A Tale of Youthing*, and the just released *LAVA LOVE – A to Z Intimacy Primer*. He explained how 'embracing of the local culture, and the people and hula and the "dance of life"... has been a big part of [his] sinking [his] roots in the soil here [laugh]' (Koob 2015).

Thinking of the future, Richard endeavours to expand Kalani's focus beyond their 'nice... little byline' of 'find yourself here' to also being able to offer the opportunity for people to 'advance yourself here'. He elaborated 'because... we get people sometimes that are lost, that are really searching for themselves, and that's wonderful, and we want to help them, but we also want to have the people that already have direction... And we're doing that [now]' (Koob 2015). This is certainly reflected in the new generation of leadership at Kalani.

Scott reflected how:

> Before I even came here... Kalani... was still kind of an enigma... And then when I got here it was kind of like a lifting of the veil on a place that is kind of a haven for bringing out the light, in people. Or a haven at least for people that want to try and practice that as their intention in this world. And a training ground for that as well. And I think through time I've come to see that more and more. And it's kind of grown more and more intense, that realisation that this is really not only a refuge for people that want to bring out the light, and create the light in this lifetime, but it's also that training ground you know, it's where we get stronger at it. And I try to live that philosophy into what we do in the Department, I try to live that philosophy in all my interactions every single day.
> (Laaback 2015)

Tiki also spoke of future plans to build a Performing Arts Centre and to keep improving Kalani,

> we're not here for the money, we're not here to further our careers… we're here because we love it and… we love the opportunity to give to it and to help it, not to, not grow so much, but [to]… raise the quality of the experience.
>
> (DeGenaro 2015)

Ali believes that,

> I think we've shifted into this new age, from my perspective anyway, where we're moving from an age where we're *talking* about the things we need to do for the planet and the things that we need to do to be sustainable, and to, protect… our natural environment that we are a part of and that we ultimately need to survive, so shifting from the talking… phase to the actually modeling it phase. And so that's what I believe is our kuleana, our responsibility here is to model that and the way that I look at it is that, this is a very experimental environment. Anyone that tells you that Kalani is this or this, this place is always changing, it HAS to change, it's part of why I think it's lasted 40 years is because it *has* allowed itself to evolve with the need of the planet… I would say that our sustainability and our permaculture efforts are somewhat experimental in the sense that we're learning how to work our natural environment and we're taking techniques from… the ancient peoples and with the modern and blending those and then testing out different ways and then seeing how it goes and course correcting… and it's not perfect, we're not perfect today, we're learning, we're learning how to be sustainable, what does that mean? And it's not just, it's also not just the plants right, it's the people too because it takes a lot of actually physical labor and manpower to let's say, grow food, or pump out three meals a day from our kitchen, manage this entire property full of people and spaces… so, what does it look like to have not only sustainability for the planet but for the people, taking care of the animals that live in our space? So it's really just kind of a multi-dimensional experiment, and, in my mind it's a question of, how do we keep making it better? And also, even bringing in a little bit of yoga philosophy, like how do we just be where we are right now, and see that where we are is perfect? And how can we, and still understanding that we do have that vision of getting even smarter and better?
>
> (Slous 2015)

For Tiki service and gratitude are vital components of Kalani's vision:

> … there's a real theme here of improving body, mind, and spirit, and also of service… when I came here as a volunteer…. I was soooo happy to

> work in our kitchen [laugh] and do dishes, and prepare food, and help the chefs, and serve the food, and... there's usually a chant before and or after, and some kind of an intention. They eat together, and it's just consciousness I think. And the consciousness of being grateful... people, if they give themselves a chance, they see that there's just a very deep enlightening experience in service. And some people in the regular, we call it the 'default world', never have the chance to experience that.... Here... we talk to our volunteers about the experience of give and take... [to] open yourself to the experience of that.... they all have a chance to really make a difference, in the minutes or the seconds that they're interacting with somebody. And I think that's a real permeating theme here. And it's beautiful.
>
> (DeGenaro 2015)

In conclusion, Tiki explained how,

> we always feel happy if somebody goes away at least knowing two words: aloha and mahalo, [laugh] and aloha and mahalo both have 'ha' in it... ha means the breath... there's so many translations for aloha, but it means hello, and goodbye, and love. And mahalo is, living in gratitude, extending your gratitude... my favorite word is imua, and imua means to move forward... no matter what, and... I love that word because it just brings me so much inspiration, even if life poses challenges...
>
> (DeGenaro 2015)

Conclusion

Members of Kalani's stories explain how Hawaiian sacred places, particularly the halau and heiau sites, have inspired the creation and use of new educational, sustainable development spaces throughout the community. Kalani's co-founders Richard and Earnest from the outset deeply respected the Hawaiian culture and people, and their retreat centre was modeled on the Hawaiian ahupua'a and 'ohana. They were ever grateful, mahalo, for the connection they felt and established with the land and local community. Following Earnest's death, his presence lives on at Kalani, embodied in beautiful photographs of him dancing and in stories recounted of his wonderful and inspiring life. Richard remains highly active within the Kalani community, encouraging a new generation of leadership to respect Hawaiian traditions and to keep growing, welcoming innovative ideas and individuals to expand and refine Kalani's programmes. Scott's Permaculture Program is a notable addition, which has created a workspace, nursery and gardens teeming with life and an educational component, to spread the message of ecologically sustainable living throughout and beyond the community.

The new leaders at Kalani also hold a deep sense of reverence and respect for nature and Hawaiian culture. They are committed to sustainable development and service, in order to continue to develop new and old ways of living in harmony with nature, of which they consider themselves to be a part. The food that Kalani serves, its many styles of yoga workshops, the arts and cultural programmes they teach, and their use of social media all exemplify this dedication. These modern tools and techniques, many of them drawn from ancient indigenous Hawaiian, Eastern and Western principles, are used to further personal and sustainable development within Kalani and the broader Puna district. They use real world and online places as educative sites, modeling an ideal society that is constantly growing and learning, responding to the needs of the planet. As noted above, it's not perfect, it's experimental, and Kalani encounters many challenges along the way. It is a political and social project, which openly questions mainstream capitalist urban life and values, yet it is also a modern business, dependent on capital and social media for its survival. It is continually seeking ethical ways to be self-sustaining, in the midst of and in response to economic and environmental crises.

The stories of Kalani's founders and community members, and the creation and use of places within Kalani are central to understanding its mission and sincere intention to create a better way of being with nature, culture, and wellness, with education and sustainability as central principles. All of Kalani, the Big Island, and indeed the earth we inhabit are considered sacred and treated as such. All are accepted as who and where they are, on their journey of self-development. These are Kalani's ideals – to create a heaven on earth – and to spread the message that it is possible and necessary to do so globally. The first step is slowing down and being there.

Notes

1 Scott Laaback, Kalani's Permaculture Manager, was interviewed for this case study and allowed his comments to be identified in this chapter. They are cited as (Laaback 2015), as the interview was conducted in 2015.
2 Richard Koob was interviewed for this case study and allowed his comments to be identified in this chapter. They are cited as (Koob 2015), as the interview was conducted in 2015.
3 Tiki DeGenaro was interviewed for this case study and allowed her comments to be identified in this chapter. They are cited as (DeGenaro 2015), as the interview was conducted in 2015.
4 Ali Slous was interviewed for this case study and allowed her comments to be identified in this chapter. They are cited as (Slous 2015), as the interview was conducted in 2015.

References

Kalani n.d. *Home*, viewed 1 February 2015, https://kalani.com.
Koob, R. 2014, *Kalani: A leap of faith, hope and love*, Kalani Publishers, Pahoa.

6 Stand Up and Muslim Sudanese women in Melbourne

Introduction

Standing on slightly raised ground one block back from the busy main high street of Dandenong is Trinity Uniting Church. This church is built in a classic Australian, late nineteenth-century style using clinker brick with thick buttresses along its exterior, and narrow deep-set stained-glass windows. Its wooden panel roof is dark and high. It has two aisles running its length from the altar to the portico at its entrance. The church is approximately 40 metres by 15 metres with twelve rows of wooden pews providing seating for a congregation of up to 300 people. In more recent times, its associated administrative buildings have been incorporated into the church structure though the annexing of open space between the original structures. So buildings that were once adjacent to the church now form part of the larger complex. The room in which the Stand Up programme takes place is one of the church buildings that now forms part of the larger single structure. In an ordinary office-like meeting room of around 4 metres by 8 metres, a group of women comes together each week. The room is furnished with rectangular tables and chairs and there is a large whiteboard at one end. Muslim women, ranging in age from their early twenties to late sixties, sit alongside mostly female Stand Up staff and volunteers,[1] completing various English language worksheets together.

For more than ten years, a Jewish aid agency called Stand Up has been working with Muslim Sudanese women in the southeast suburb of Dandenong, which is located in metropolitan Melbourne, Australia. The community development activities associated within this partnership have, over the last three years, been occurring within a Christian church. Given the historical and contemporary tensions between Jewish and Muslim communities, this assistance does at first appear unexpected, even more so when the location of this programme is considered. Indeed, this conflation of a Jewish agency, working with Muslim women in a Christian church is relatively unique within the Australian context, yet despite what may be considered an unexpected triumvirate, the community development activities occurring within this environment are quite successful. Focusing primarily on English language training and supportive social networks, as well as providing other welfare-based services to these women and their families, this programme addresses a range of needs self-identified by the Sudanese women as they and their families resettle in Australia.

To understand how this partnership has succeeded, it is important to understand the history of the Jewish aid agency Stand Up, the socio-economic circumstances and migration patterns of Dandenong, as well as the past usage of the church building currently housing these activities. In fact, the success of this community development collaboration is in large part an artefact of these separate historic trajectories. These circumstances therefore in which Jews and Muslims meet in a Christian church are very specific to this location, which in large part allows this community development project to achieve its goals.

Union of separate trajectories

Stand Up

Known today as Stand Up, this community development organisation was originally formed under the name Keshet in direct response to the Rwanda crisis in 1994. Previous to the establishment of Keshet, there was no such aid agency within Australia with direct links to the Jewish community. Raising more than AUD40,000 within a single week, Keshet signaled that the Melbourne Jewish community wanted an organisation through which they could actively engage with the international aid sector (JAA 2012). This generous and immediate response to the horrific humanitarian disaster unfolding in Rwanda at that time, and the commitment to social justice within the Jewish community should not be unexpected. According to Rabbi David Rosen, Executive Director of a similar US-based aid agency called *AVODAH*, 'it's not random that so many Jews are involved in social justice. People are motivated to act politically by their core values. They act politically, not out of economic self-interest, but as a community anchored in a powerful set of values' (JAA 2011, p. 20). The Jewish religion is one that identifies with the most vulnerable in society and prioritises a charitable response to the needs of others (see Clarke 2011, 2013 for fuller discussion of links between Judaism and development theory and practice). Judaism is also a hopeful religion, but one that demands God's justice for all. Through its own difficult history of persecution, Judaism reflects that as God's chosen people, there is a responsibility to share God's love with others. As a very practical religion, it also makes clear, for example, the role and value of charity to support those who are in need (Leaman 2006). Establishing an aid agency to facilitate this practical expression of their religious duties and beliefs was therefore not unexpected when faced with the humanitarian crisis in Rwanda.

As Keshet grew, its name changed in 2004 to Jewish Aid Australia (JAA) to more clearly articulate its mission and purpose of 'mobilising the Jewish community's resources and networks towards empowering vulnerable communities'. At this time, the agency also increased its professionalisation by employing its first staff member. While welcoming assistance and support from all Australians, JAA purposely sought to maintain its identity as a Jewish organisation by firmly rooting its approach to community development in its religious teaching. Through this religious anchoring, JAA was important to the entire Jewish community, receiving support from progressive communities to more orthodox communities within Melbourne (and later Australia) as it provided an opportunity to practically express key Jewish values and commitments. As stated in a recent JAA Annual Report (2012, p. 5):

> Through our work, JAA realises the Jewish values of *chessed* (Kindness), *tzedek* (Justice) and *tikkun olam* (Repairing the World). We hope to inspire the Australian Jewish community to fulfill these obligations in their everyday lives.

In 2012, JAA changed its name to Stand Up. This rebranding was not to disassociate itself from its Jewish heritage, but rather aimed at rebranding and refreshing the organisation to be better positioned within a crowded fundraising marketplace. Part of this rebranding was to also allow the agency to re-state very clearly its goals and mission. As such, Stand Up defines itself as being involved in engagement, education and empowerment. While it receives some government financial support, the majority of its work is community funded with ancillary support through various philanthropic trusts. Whilst formed in response to the crisis in Rwanda, Stand Up almost immediately began to also undertake fundraising for community development work within Australia. Its early annual appeals focused on homeless youth in Melbourne, Indigenous education, foster care of Melbourne children, and aged care. Later on, it raised funds for domestic disasters including bushfires and floods. Over this period it also raised funds to support crises in Papua New Guinea, Southern Africa and Turkey, as well as refugees from Kosovo and East Timor resettling in Australia. By 2015 it had more than 20 staff operating activities in Victoria, New South Wales and Western Australia with an annual budget approaching AUD1 million (JAA 2012).

Some of its early programmes grew out of a global fundraising campaign – 'Save Darfur' – initially coordinated through the World Jewish Service. These first programmes were largely focused on material assistance to arriving refugees from this region. As personal relationships were built between Stand Up staff and volunteers and these community members, the English language training needs of women became apparent and so Stand Up began to offer organised classes in response. Thus in 2004, Stand Up began to implement more longer-term community development activities with local communities and a year later began its work with Sudanese refugees located in Dandenong.

Dandenong

The city of Greater Dandenong is located 25 kilometres to the south-east of Melbourne (the capital city of the State of Victoria, Australia). The population of this centre is approximately 150,000 with projections of 16 per cent growth in the next ten years (CGD 2015). Greater Dandenong is the most culturally diverse municipality in Victoria, and the second most diverse in Australia, with residents from over 150 different birthplaces, well over half (60 per cent) of its population have been born overseas, and 55 per cent from nations where English is not the main spoken language. Birthplaces include Vietnam, Cambodia, Sri Lanka, India, China, Italy, Greece, Bosnia, Afghanistan, New Zealand and Britain (CGD 2015). The population of Dandenong is expected to grow in the coming years, but such population growth will continue the recent history of population trends. Much of this growth has been the result of recently arrived migrants moving to this location. Between 2006 and 2011, overseas born residents in the City of Greater Dandenong rose by 20 per cent with more than 6,000 Indian-born residents, nearly 2,000 Sri Lankans, 1,100 Vietnamese and 900 Afghans moving into the area (CGD 2015). Residents that had arrived in earlier waves of migration, including from the United Kingdom, Croatia, Greece and Italy, also declined during this same period further exaggerating the ever-changing multicultural make-up of Dandenong.

In terms of its economic base, Dandenong was traditionally a site of manufacturing, with the largest employer in the area being an automotive assembly line. With economic reforms and subsequent structural changes over the past three decades, this prominence of local manufacturing underpinning the local economy has waned resulting in lower socio-economic circumstances than previously experienced. With limited local employment opportunities, the median weekly gross income of residents within the City of Greater Dandenong is the lowest across metropolitan Melbourne at around two-thirds of the average for all of Melbourne. While unemployment rates fluctuate across the state of Victoria, Dandenong has generally reported rates of more than 3–4 per cent higher than the state average. Youth unemployment has also been historically higher in Dandenong compared to the wider state, with high school completion rates also lagging behind state averages. Crime rates in Dandenong are also significantly higher than the Melbourne average with overall offences being around 40 per cent higher than the Melbourne average, with drug offences more than 85 per cent higher, and with violent offences and property offences both being greater than 75 per cent higher. Indeed, the rates of violent offences in Dandenong are the highest in metropolitan Melbourne outside the central district business area (in which there is a great concentration of licensed venues). Within Dandenong the patronage of poker machines is also problematic with the area experiencing the highest rates of gambling losses in Victoria, with more than two billion Australian dollars lost to gambling machines since their introduction just over three decades ago. Dandenong also has a higher ratio of people renting their homes than other parts of metropolitan Melbourne with more than a third of households renting accommodation (CGD 2015).

As noted in the 2011 Australian Bureau of Statistics Socio-Economic Indexes for Areas, Measures of Disadvantage scale, the municipality of Greater Dandenong 'has an index of 895 which ranks it at number 1 in level of disadvantage among the municipalities of Victoria – placing it among the most disadvantaged in the state' (CGD 2015). Within this challenging socio-economic environment, there are also a high proportion of recently arrived migrants to Australia, attracted by the less expensive rental market but also to a community that is now very culturally diverse in make-up. For example, of the families with children living in Dandenong, three-quarters of these parents were born overseas (CGD 2015). Such a rich ethnic diversity does, as would be expected, also result in religious diversity. While half of all Dandenong residents self-report as Christian, the proportion who self-report as Buddhist (18 per cent), Muslim (11 per cent) or Hindu (4 per cent) are far greater than in other parts of metropolitan Melbourne (CGD 2015).

Many of these recent migrants are asylum seekers, with Dandenong having the largest number of asylum seekers residing within its boundaries compared to any other municipality within Victoria. Almost one-third of all irregular maritime arrivals on Bridging E Visas reside in Dandenong. Of these, the overwhelming majority are male (over 80 per cent), with one-third of all asylum seekers in this visa category originating in Iran, just under a quarter from Sri Lanka, and Afghanistan being the other major originating country. Sudanese migrants, whilst small comparatively, are an important sub-community within Dandenong, with more than 1,000 people born in Sudan now living there. Unemployment within this group is very high with more than one-third not currently working. Those that are working are doing so predominantly within the field of laboring, resulting in their median wage being lower than even the already low median wage across the Dandenong area. On such low wages, it is not surprising that 90 per cent of these Sudanese migrants are renting their homes. While the overwhelming proportion of these migrants self-report as Christian, 15 per cent self-report as Muslim (CGD 2015). It is with this smaller sub-group of Sudanese refugees that Stand Up partners.

Trinity Uniting Church

The first European settlement in Dandenong was around 1837. This site was quite isolated from the then small town of Melbourne and took a full day's travel by bullock-cart traversing rough, though generally flat, tracks. By 1854, there were sufficient European settlers (predominantly small-scale farmers and grazers) that Dandenong was noted as a village with a number of permanent buildings and shops. The first recorded Methodist service was held in 1855 and in 1868, the first wooden chapel was replaced by a brick structure – which in turn was replaced by the present Trinity Church structure in 1887. It remained the primary place of worship for Methodists in Dandenong until 1977 when the Congregational Union of Australia, the Presbyterian Church of Australia, and the Methodist Church of Australasia formed the Uniting Church. For nearly 30 years now, this Church has therefore been home to this amalgamated congregation within the Dandenong region.

Working with migrant families within the Dandenong area is not new for those associated with the Trinity Uniting Church (Campbell and Oldmeadow

2006). The Church Immigration Committee was established in 1959, initially sponsoring families from the UK and later refugee families from (now former) Yugoslavia. Soon after (primarily due to the government migration services being located in this location), migrants and refugees from many other countries were welcomed by this church-based service. Families from Holland, Hungary, Austria, Egypt, Albania, Lebanon, Armenia, Mauritius, Chile, Romania, France, Germany, Assyria, Bulgaria, China, Afghanistan, Spain, India and Greece were all assisted in various ways. This support included the church paying and guaranteeing rent for housing, meeting arrivals at the Port and bringing them to Dandenong, organising interpreters when required, providing furnishings for their homes, delivering food, and assisting with gaining employment in nearby manufacturing industries.

In this regard, the church and associated church buildings have also been used for a wide variety of community endeavours, including acting as meeting places for the local YWCA, art exhibitions, drama performances, the horticultural society, mothers' clubs, Alcoholics Anonymous, Country Women's Association, Bible study groups, Scouts, and for wedding receptions and birthday parties (Campbell and Oldmeadow 2006). The Trinity Uniting Church has also been a longtime member of the local Interfaith Network within Dandenong that has as its creed: 'Many Faiths, One People'. This Network has been acknowledged for its best practices in promoting positive interfaith relations within and beyond the city of Melbourne, including a highly praised tour of diverse places of worship (Halafoff 2013). It is within this church room that Stand Up conducts its community development programmes with local Muslim Sudanese women.

Community development activities

The journey of Stand Up and the Muslim women working together within the Trinity Uniting Christian church occurred sometime after Stand Up began partnering with the Sudanese community in Dandenong. As discussed above, Stand Up initially focused primarily on support programmes being implemented by other organisations (including other non-Jewish FBOs). Over time, as Stand Up grew, it began to implement its own programmes including working with the Sudanese community in Dandenong.

A recent Annual Report describes the journey and current relationship Stand Up has with this community of Sudanese Muslim women as follows:

> [Stand Up] was active in the Save Darfur movement in 2004 and 2005 and began building a strong friendship with the Darfuri community in Melbourne. The leaders requested support from the Jewish community, not just in creating awareness about the dire situation in Darfur, but to also assist the refugees learn English, find jobs and integrate into their new home.
>
> We work with two Sudanese groups in particular: those from Darfur and those from the Nuba Mountains. These groups are some of the most vulnerable communities in Australia who experience isolation along with social and

> financial hardship. Our programs, which are developed in partnership with Sudanese leaders, provide opportunities for capacity building and empowerment.
>
> These communities have been hard to reach for many agencies but they have come to trust [Stand Up] as a unique service-provider based on a friendship that has been developed over seven years. We tailor our programs specifically to the evolving needs of the communities. We do this through regular communication with participants and in consultation with community leaders.
>
> Our programs are holistic and reach a majority of community members, including women, men and children.
>
> (JAA 2012, p. 21)

Soon after the initial programme began, the Sudanese women identified the need for sewing classes in their community. Stand Up approached another service provider – Mission Australia – who made available a purpose built space in Dandenong that allowed the teaching of sewing skills. This facility had multiple sewing machines, and large cutting tables and so forth. Stand Up at that time employed a professional sewing teacher. Within a short period however, the local Council redeveloped the buildings in which this facility was housed meaning that Stand Up had to seek a new premises to conduct this community development programme.

The geographical area in which it was practical to run this activity was quite limited. It had to be close enough to the city-centre of Dandenong that women who relied on public transport from a range of locations could easy travel to it. It also could not be a fully commercial space due to funding constraints. At this time, the refurbishments of the Trinity Unity Church, which included the covered annex of church and church buildings, were completed and Stand Up was welcomed by the Church minister to utilise these new church buildings and facilities. Indeed, Stand Up was the first community group to use these new buildings following the refurbishments. The refurbishment of the buildings made for a very welcoming environment. The carpets were new and clean, the kitchen and bathroom facilities were all in excellent order, and the furnishings were comfortable. It was a very modern and attractive space that bolstered the sense of value of both Stand Up and the women participating in the programme. It was certainly far more attractive than the previous building they were using (Staff Member A 2015).

One of the Stand Up staff members did state that '[w]hen we started, there was some tension' in our community, about a Jewish organisation working with women from a Muslim community. However, the ongoing project was described to have aided in 'overcoming barriers' of such work. They also thought that perhaps some volunteers did not initially share their involvement in this activity with their family and friends due to concerns they might have with the programme (Staff Member B 2015). However, none of the (long-term) volunteers interviewed described having such experiences, instead they were very positive about their involvement in this programme and did not reflect any concerns with its cross-faith engagement component.

As discussed briefly above, the Trinity Uniting Church was very ecumenical in its outlook and has welcomed many external groups to utilise their buildings for places of worship outside Christian denominations. An example of this was allowing a Bat Mitzvah to take place in the church hall. This Jewish ceremony celebrates a young woman entering adulthood in Judaism. In this particular instance, the traditional Synagogue and family celebration was eschewed in favour of a community celebration involving the North Sudanese community as a display of connection between these two communities. Similarly, the Church has also hosted weekend cross-cultural experiences with children from the Jewish community spending the day there listening to speakers from the North Sudanese community explain about their faith and culture (Staff Member A 2015).

From the Stand Up institutional perspective, the Trinity Uniting Church is a community space that aids their work with the North Sudanese women. It is considered by Stand Up as much more than physical space. As one of their staff members described: ‘It is a warm welcoming space that breaks down barriers’ (Staff Member D 2015). Another staff member also remarked that it was not ‘cold and sterile’ as would a more secular space be (Staff Member A 2015). As many denominations are regularly welcomed and can make use of the Trinity Church’s spaces, the choice of the Trinity Uniting Church was not an issue for Stand Up staff or for the Sudanese women. Indeed, for many of the Stand Up volunteers and Muslim women, the location of the community development activities was actually seen to enhance the outcomes and foster strong participation. While there is no mistaking that the Church is a place of Christian worship, this has not been a barrier for Jewish or Muslim participation. By contrast, it is part of its attraction to both organisers and participants. As a Stand Up staff member noted, similarly to their colleague above: ‘It is a safe space that you go into. For women who have arrived in Australia as refugees, they feel safe and secure in this environment. It is a space without barriers’ (Staff Member C 2015).

As such, each Thursday, at midday, a two-hour programme centring on English language training coordinated by a Stand Up staff member and supported by volunteers begins. (It finishes by 3.00 p.m. to allow women with child-rearing responsibilities to collect school-aged children). During the period of observational fieldwork, around 20 women attended weekly meetings to undertake English language training and social networking and support. Whilst the timetable for the activities was set, women arrived throughout the three-hour period. Some of the women arrived by private car, some by public bus and others walked. On occasion, the number of women was much lower (with just six participating on the second site visit and with four of them arriving one hour into the three-hour activity). These English language classes are run by a qualified teacher and supported by up to ten Stand Up volunteers. The number of volunteers can also vary from week to week with some volunteers participating each week and others attending on a more ad hoc basis depending on their other commitments. During these language classes, childcare is provided in a room adjacent to the working space, though some children prefer to stay with their mothers.

An example of this English language training was how to book a doctor's appointment. The teacher worked through a prepared script and then in small groups the women and volunteers practiced the dialogue. An extension exercise associated with this lesson was how to make such requests in a polite manner with the teacher demonstrating which words used portrayed 'polite conversation'. Part of the dialogue also included the women expressing a preference for female doctors. It was evident that there were different levels of English language ability with the group, from basic to near fluent. English/Arabic dictionaries were also available as a resource to assist this activity and the women were encouraged to take the 'scripts' home with them for their own use. During the role-play and discussions of small groups, there was much laughter and joking. It was clear that there is a genuine friendship between the women and volunteers. They met each other warmly with hugs and kisses. They spontaneously asked about each other's families and shared stories and gave updates about these personal aspects of their lives. As they waited for activities to start, they didn't segregate into 'women' and 'volunteers' but naturally mixed with one another.

In addition to the English training classes, there is value in providing childcare for these women so they can also have some time socialising with other women from their community. As noted, these women have young children and limited opportunities to engage in community-based activities outside their own homes. Therefore, as a Stand Up staff member described, 'this is a time for them to meet their friends and have a coffee while someone else takes care of their children' (Staff Member C 2015). In addition, each week, the women can purchase (halal) meals for themselves and their family at AUD1 per meal plus unlimited fruit. These meals are supplied free of charge by another welfare charity.

Thus, activities that occur within the Stand Up programme address multiple needs. In addition to the English language classes and social support for mothers, there are also training for Sudanese community members to establish and run their own community groups, holiday programmes for Sudanese youth, homework clubs, social outings for the wider Sudanese community, mentoring programmes to provide individual Sudanese families with a volunteer to assist them with navigating unfamiliar bureaucracies and other resettlement tasks, and financial support for vocational training, as well as the facilitation of placements for Sudanese women undertaking training, such as in aged care. Indeed, Stand Up has organised work experience for North Sudanese women undertaking formal study in areas such as aged care and disability care through other Jewish welfare organisations. For example, there are now currently six Sudanese women working in Jewish aged care facilities. Thus, there is now a situation in which these survivors of Darfur are now caring for survivors of the Holocaust. Much of the Jewish community in Melbourne were themselves refugees following World War II, and so an affinity around these experiences may very well aid relationships that on the surface appear unlikely. Further, in addition to this direct work with the Dandenong Sudanese community, Stand Up also implements an advocacy programme called Nuba Now. This programme was launched in 2012 with the aim of raising awareness about the continuing crisis in the Nuba Mountains of Sudan. The 2012 JAA Annual Report states that 'Nuba Now is based on three foundational pillars: raising awareness, raising funds and igniting political change' (p. 18). Recognising their own institutional boundaries, Stand Up partnered with a larger aid agency, CARE Australia, to deliver the in-country programmes.

Reflections on development spaces

In speaking with both members of the Sudanese community and Stand Up's Jewish volunteers, the location within a Christian church building of the community development activities is neither seen as a negative nor as an inhibitor of participation or success. As one volunteer noted, it 'makes no difference that we are operating within Church buildings. There is no difference. It is just a building as far as I am concerned. I don't feel uncomfortable here at all. The other volunteers feel the same as I do' (Volunteer C 2015). Another volunteer similarly stated:

> We are all one human family. If people (other volunteers) had a problem then they would not have come. Just like the women. They come for the activities, not for anything spiritual, so it doesn't matter that it is a church. In the room in which we met, there are Jews, Muslims, Buddhists, Hindus and Christians. It doesn't matter what the building is.
>
> (Volunteer D 2015)

Participant D (2015) felt a certain affinity, given that Christian churches were places in which God is revered and also felt no disharmony with her own faith tradition: 'There are no problems meeting in a Christian church. Even though we are different religions, we are all worshiping the same God. It doesn't matter I am meeting in a church as I always stay a Muslim.'

For others, the sacred nature of the building as a setting for community development played a more pronounced positive role in the achievement of community development goals. Participant B (2015) stated: 'The church is different to a library or another building. The church is always quiet and if you want to pray you can just go and pray and no-one will say anything to you.' Another woman noted, 'the actual building does matter. At church you feel peaceful, safe and you respect the place' (Participant A 2015).

Indeed, at times some of the Muslim women would leave the activity they were involved in, unfold their prayer mat and undertake their daily prayers. Given the orientation of the buildings, these women would be kneeling at the base of the Church wall adjacent to its altar facing Mecca.

For both volunteers and participants, Christian churches were not unfamiliar. As one Muslim woman said, 'I have been to a Christian church before for a funeral' (Participant A 2015). Or as another recounted, 'my father's family has Christians in it and so I have visited churches before for weddings and other celebrations. So it is ok for me to visit here and not be uncomfortable' (Participant D 2015). In a similar vein, a volunteer noted, 'I have been to Christian churches before for weddings, funerals and so on' (Volunteer B 2015). But, the women also stated that attending a Christian church building for a non-religious event was unusual: 'I had been to a wedding in a Christina church but this is the first time I have been to a church for anything other than a wedding' (Participant D 2015). Given that Australia is a Christian majority country, this is not so surprising, while the Jewish volunteers were much less familiar with mosques, and the Muslim participants were much less familiar with synagogues.

A number of the Sudanese women interviewed also made it clear that their families were supportive of their participation in the Stand Up programme regardless of the fact it was run by a Jewish aid agency within a Christian Church: 'My family understand. My husband does not mind that I am meeting in a church with Jewish women' (Participant B 2015). Similar comments were made by others about their own and their partner's perspective, including, 'I feel comfortable in the church because I respect all religions. My husband is happy for me to come as he also respects all religions' (Participant C 2015), and 'as a Muslim, I believe in Christianity and do not feel threatened by their beliefs. My husband is fine with me coming to a Christian church' (Participant E 2015).

Indeed the location of this activity within the Christian church building may have facilitated participation for some women, as the location of the activity in some measure lessened anxiety some Muslim women had in being involved with a Jewish organisation – an anxiety linked to the limited exposure to Judaism in Sudan. Having been part of the programme these anxieties were lessened and they developed a more positive understanding of Jewish people and culture.

> Before I came to Australia I had different understanding of Jewish people. In Australia it is ok to talk with Jewish women. I now have a better understanding of Jewish people.
>
> (Participant G 2015)

> Before I came to Australia I didn't know any Jewish people. Now I have a different understanding that Jewish people are good people who look after the poor.
>
> (Participant B 2015)

> I was angry with my friend when she told me what she was doing with these Jewish women. Muslims and Jews have much conflict. But I soon learned there was no conflict here (Participant F 2015).
>
> This would not happen in my home country (North Sudan). But it is good to have different experiences.
>
> (Participant D 2015)

The implementation of these programmes for this cohort of Muslim Sudanese women certainly filled a need that was not being met by other service providers. As Participant C (2015) described:

> When I arrived in Australia I couldn't speak English. A volunteer (from Stand Up) would visit my house each week and help me. Then I started coming to these meetings every week. I wanted to learn English plus other new things. With Stand Up we go different places each week. We have been to the Aquarium, Museum, Bunnings [hardware store chain] for classes on how to fix things around the house. We have also learned knitting, typing and computers. With this group I would not have had these experiences or visited these places with my children.

Such activities aren't currently offered through organisations in the local area associated with the Muslim women's own faith, which are not as well established or resourced as the Melbourne Jewish communities. As Participant A (2015) noted: 'No activities like this happen in mosques. In mosques the ethnic groups stick together.' Or as another woman stated: 'There are no programmes like this in my mosque. Muslims stay in ethnic groups in the mosques. I do go to the mosques on Fridays but there are no free activities like this' (Participant B 2015). Indeed, much of the benefits of this programme are the socialisation opportunities provided to these Muslim women.

> I don't need to come for English lessons anymore. But my child (19 months old) likes playing with the other children. I help in the childcare during the English lessons and then talk with the other women afterwards during the activities.
>
> (Participant B 2015)

> I was told about it by one of my friends. I like being able to meet with my friends here each week.
>
> (Participant C 2015)

> People come here for peace. We come here to learn English and socialise. I can see my friends here. It is exciting for me to be part of this.
>
> (Participant F 2015)

The English lessons are very practical and assist these women to navigate day to day events and they also provide a basis for further learning. As one of the Sudanese participants stated, 'I want to also help people. I have a dream to be a nurse so I can help those who are sick' (Participant A 2015). For her, the English language classes were the first step in achieving this goal. There is clearly also cultural exchange happening over the course of this community development programme. Even the experience of tasting food associated with one culture or the other builds up the relationships between the volunteers and Muslim women. As one Muslim woman said, 'Challah is now my favourite bread. I first tried it at a Stand Up event. When I had my last baby, this was the food I wanted to eat straight away and I asked the volunteers to bring some to the hospital for me' (Participant B 2015).

The strength and sincerity of relationships built up between participants and volunteers are highly evident. 'There is lots of respect shown between the women and the volunteers' was how one volunteer described it (Volunteer A 2015). This may be because there are similar refugee experiences between these two cohorts. Again, a long-term Stand Up volunteer noted, 'I can identify with their refugee experiences. I came to Australia as a 21-year-old woman with nothing. I never saw my mother again and had to start a new life here' (Volunteer C 2015). This connection is extremely powerful and underscores that the differences in religion can be overcome by the similarities of such experiences and with the assistance of strong interfaith networks committed to helping those in need.

Conclusion

On the surface, it does seem a very unlikely scenario in which successful community development outcomes might be achieved: a Jewish aid agency working alongside Muslim women within a Christian church. Yet it is precisely this combination of organisation, people and location that is delivering valuable community development goals.

While Stand Up as a Jewish aid agency was working with these Muslim Sudanese women in a more traditional secular space prior to the relocation to the current Christian church building, it was noted by a number of participants and volunteers that the church building was a factor in the programme maintaining its level of engagement with the Muslim women. While there have been some limited excursions to Jewish sites, including a day-trip to a non-Orthodox synagogue, to enhance cultural exchange, the use of a Christian church building has facilitated an environment in which Jews and Muslims can partner with one another. As noted by a number of participants, such community development activities are currently not available within local mosques in the area. Nor are there any synagogues in or near Dandenong, providing such facilities, whereas the Christian church was ideally located near the major public transport hubs of Dandenong and thus easily accessible by public transport from the suburbs in which these women live. This mix of ideal location and religious independence thus provided not only a safe space for Stand Up and Muslim women to gather to undertake various community development programmes, but according to those involved, actually enhanced the outcomes of this programme.

In this instance, the importance of the sacred place of the church building was that it added to the sense of religious equality between the aid agency and the participants. To use a clumsy sporting analogy, the Christian church did not provide a 'home-ground advantage' to either group, but was sufficiently familiar as to make both groups feel a sense of belonging and security. Of course, as discussed previously, not all of those involved identified the church building as playing such an active role, but when asked, the majority of Stand Up staff, volunteers and participants did identify the building itself as having a material positive impact on the programme. While not actively engaged in this particular activity, it is worthy to note that the various lay and ordained Church members who were regularly present during the Thursday afternoon activities did not consider this use of church buildings as inappropriate, but rather viewed these activities by these users as expected and normal within their church. Thus, for the 'owners' of this sacred place, the undertaking of community development activities was most certainly appropriate use of the space. Stand Up was inspired by their Jewish religious teachings to provide assistance to those in need, in this case the Sudanese Muslim community with settlement into Australian life and culture. The Trinity Uniting Church also enabled the Stand Up programme to be delivered on the basis of their shared religious teachings' commitment to help one's neighbour.

It is of course not possible to fully know what may have happened to this programme had the relocation to the Trinity Uniting Church been instead to another council owned building. While the programme may well have continued to thrive within a 'secular place', the Stand Up staff, volunteers and participants did make clear that from their perspective the sacred nature of the church building in which they were working was a positive force in the success of their programme. From their perspective, the location of a Jewish aid agency working with Muslim women within a Christian church building was not a novelty but rather, in the context in which they were working, a core component aiding the achievement of their community development goals. So whilst neither the agency nor the community 'owned' this particular sacred place – its inherent sacredness did play an observable role in being a successful development space, particularly in the city of Dandenong, which is noted as a centre for interfaith activities.

Note

1 Seven Stand Up Participants, four Staff Members and four Volunteers' anonymised comments are included in the chapter and cited as (Participant A-G 2015), (Staff Member A-D) and (Volunteer A-D), as the interviews were conducted in 2015.

References

Campbell, N. & Oldmeadow, M. 2006, *Tall tress to Trinity*, mimeo. Trinity Uniting Church, Dandenong.

City of Greater Dandenong (CDG) 2015, *Statistical data for Victorian communities, Summary of social conditions in greater Dandenong*, viewed 20 October 2015, http://www.greaterdandenong.com/document/18464/statistical-data-for-victorian-communities.

Clarke, M. 2011, *Development and religion*, Edward Elgar, Cheltenham.

Clarke, M. 2013, 'Judaism – A Cry for Help', in M. Clarke (ed.), *Handbook of research on religion and development*, Edward Elgar, London.

Halafoff, A. 2013, *The multifaith movement: Global risks and cosmopolitan solutions*. Springer, Dordrecht.

Jewish Aid Australia (JAA) 2012, *Annual Report 2012: Connecting the Dots*, viewed 8 October 2015, https://jewishaidaustralia.files.wordpress.com/2012/11/jaa-annual-report-2012.pdf.

Leaman, O. 2006, *Jewish thought*, Routledge, New York.

7 Conclusion: bridging theory and practice around place and space

Sacred places are common. They can be found across the world, from large metropolises to small remote towns and villages. Often, these religious structures dominate the landscape and are built as expressions of religious faith. Across the world, many of the iconic buildings we associate with specific countries and travel to visit and admire (and photograph) are religious places of worship. These places can be hundreds of years old and remain the only structures from periods of time long past. Not all sacred places are physical though with some places of worship being located within the natural world. Whether small or large, old or new, great or modest – these sacred places can evoke a sense of awe and wonder for those of the same faith, different faith or even no faith.

Given the large proportion of the world's population that profess religious belief – 8.5 people out of 10 (Pew 2012) – it is not surprising that places for religious worship are so commonplace. Those with religious belief need not only somewhere to practice their religion and worship but for many religious people, the building of religious structures forms part of their religious adherence (Clarke 2011). As this volume has illustrated through a number of case studies though, these religious buildings and places are utilised for many more activities than simply worship. Whether in developed or developing nations, these religious places are locations where local communities congregate for purposes beyond just religious rituals.

With more than one billion people continuing to live in or near poverty (World Bank 2015), it is on one hand not surprising that initiatives seeking to improve the lives of the poor occur within these places. Again, whether in developed or developing countries, religious places often house community development activities that range from disaster relief and response, to formal and informal education services, to gender equality and environmental awareness programmes. The need to improve the lives of the poor remains overwhelming, while at the same time caring for societies' most vulnerable can be found at the core of all of the world's major religions, as can the imperative to work on personal development and for social justice more broadly. On the other hand, it could also be seen as somewhat incongruous that these purpose-built places would be used for such non-worship purposes. Moreover, it is not immediately intuitive that such places would benefit from the achievement of community development outcomes. Closer examination though, as has occurred within the case studies contained within this volume, do make clear that there are common effects of these religious places that do engender feelings of trust, belonging, openness, and authority that enhance the achievement of these outcomes.

Indeed, the argument is made that the theory of community development has not kept pace with its practice in this regard around the intersection of space and place. Unlike in other disciplines or fields of research, community development theory has been largely silent on places and spaces with regards to their impact on improving the lives of the poor and on environmental sustainability. Whilst long-standing best practice has presumed that community development activities should take place locally and within non-threatening and familiar spaces, little attention has been given to ideas of how place and space are constructed, how they interact, and how they will inevitably affect community development outcomes. This volume has hopefully contributed to what should become a much larger theoretical and practical discussion within community development by focusing on the use of sacred places for development activities. More work is clearly required on the larger consideration of the poetics and politics of place, space and development.

Theories on development, place and space

The places in which development activities occur do affect the outcomes achieved. Further consideration of this dynamic between place and space is required within development theory (and practice). Places of course should not solely be restricted to considerations of physical structures but also include virtual places and natural environments.

The case studies examined in this volume demonstrate that religious organisations and spiritual communities in economically poorer and richer contexts are addressing the Sustainable Development Goals of alleviating poverty, and improving gender equality and environmental sustainability, in places that are sacred to them and the communities that they are partnering with. The development activities occurring in these places are responsive to both local and global risks, and are conducted at once at the everyday grassroots level, and on a broader global scale in the 'real world' and also online.

While religion is often perceived as a source of conflict and tension in contemporary societies, and attacks on the validity of religion in secular societies is frequent, this volume has focused largely on the positive contributions of religion and spirituality in addressing local and global risks and advancing social and environmentally sustainable development. In so doing, our case studies have explored the 'reciprocity in the network of relations' between religion, environment and society (Kong 1990, p. 358). We have endeavoured to go beyond the Western Christian bias used for understanding religion and its relationship to sacred places, which has long dominated geographical studies of religion (Kong 1990), and instead we have examined case studies of diverse religious and spiritual contexts. In so doing, while we have included 'world religion' Christian,

Buddhist, Muslim and Jewish cases, we have also investigated a multifaith initiative and a more holistic spiritual community.

We have also followed Kong's (2001, p. 226) advice to look beyond the 'officially sacred' church, temple and mosque sites and have also explored: indigenous sacred sites; religious schools; religious halls; shrines; dance and yoga studios; organic, temple and permaculture gardens; and virtual spaces. We have endeavoured to explore 'sensuous sacred geographies' by describing not only what we saw in the field and online but also what we heard and smelled and what our participants experienced in these sacred settings. We have contextualised our case studies within 'historical and place-specific analysis' and also looked for common themes emerging from a wide range of diverse settings.

While scholars have been quick to posit that we are now living in a post-secular society, we tend to agree with Kong's (2010, p. 765) scepticism regarding the assertion that we are experiencing a re-emergence of religion at the turn of the twenty-first century and that post secularisation is occurring in 'a globalizing and totalizing way'. Not only is 'an abiding spirituality' persisting 'in the face of modernity', as Kong suggests, but in places it is a potent force being used to assist those in need and to spread an awareness that there is more to life than the fruits that capitalism promises yet seldom delivers equally. This is evident, for example, in the Minhaj-ul-Quran International's (MQI) activities centred around sacred Sufi shrines and in Kalani's Hawaiian culture, permaculture, and yoga programmes focused on personal and sustainable development.

Regarding the poetics of place, contemporary scholars of religion have been quick to dismiss substantial definitions of religion in which places are themselves possessed of sacred power that is revealed to humans. However, our research suggests that this is an area that is perhaps worthy of further investigation, considering not only Christian but a range of religious, spiritual and non-religious worldviews, and cognisant of 'the nonhuman turn' (Grusin 2015) that the social sciences and other disciplines are currently experiencing. It follows that situational definitions that locate the sacred primarily in terms of social construction and processes of sacralisation can be seen as anthropocentric. Lived experiences of our participants point to the sacred as occurring beneath and beyond mere human construction. At the same time, many of their stories describe the ways in which their sacred places have been sacralised over time by association with remarkable people and their sacred teachings and/or ritualised activities. The meanings of the places we have examined also continue to be developed and changed by the people who are creating and using them. We argue therefore that perhaps both substantial *and* situational definitions may play a crucial role in better understanding sacred spaces, at least as they are actually experienced by their communities.

The politics of places we explored no doubt provides further evidence that they are powerful not only due to their sacred meanings but also through their ownership, use and appropriation. Interestingly, these places were at times less exclusive than expected – Stand Up provided services in a Christian church to Muslim women, the MQI spaces were developed to deliver programmes not just for Muslims but for all of humanity, and Kalani welcomed and celebrated diversity, with acceptance of difference being one of their central principles. It is also worthy to note how the bhikkhunis and nuns of Songdhammakalyani Monastery (SDKM) are resisting exclusion of women in Buddhism by building and consecrating sacred places named after eminent Buddhist women, and in which statues of them occupied prominent positions. Moving these figures from the periphery to the centre, from the outside to the inside, the bhikkhunis were both being 'disruptive' to existing patriarchal structure and 'integrative' by placing women on an equal footing with men in Buddhism (Chidester and Linenthal 1995; Lane 2002, p. 48). Similarly, Kalani's permaculture programme seeks to create an alternative to capitalist modernisation, where the 'liberating intentions' of its architect (Foucault quoted in Rabinow 1984, p. 246), the Permaculture Manager, are both leading and coinciding with the practices of the Kalani community that is increasingly prioritising sustainable development. These examples well illustrate how space is certainly 'fundamental in any exercise of power' (Foucault quoted in Rabinow 1984, p. 252).

Many of the sacred places we visited were indeed 'nodal points' within much larger 'spatial networks' (Soja 1989, pp. 149, 151) that intersected with race, ethnicity and gender (Chidester and Linenthal 1995). The Presbyterian Women's Missionary Union (PWMU) exists throughout Vanuatu. SDKM is part of the global Buddhist women's network, which has a significant real and virtual presence. Stand Up enables development activities within and beyond Australia in cooperation with other aid organisations and the Minaj Welfare Foundation within MQI is also an international organisation providing welfare support in and beyond Pakistan. The sacred places we studied are also 'entangled with the entrepreneurial, the social, the political, and other "profane" forces' (Chidester and Linenthal 1995, p. 16) as evidenced by Kalani's Steward Program and MQI's action-seeking political reform in Pakistan.

Hybridity is also evident in many of the cases we documented as different waves of colonisation and migration in diverse settings have created complex relations among people and places. Contestation over these sites was seldom mentioned by participants in this study, who rather spoke of how newer religious or spiritual communities highly respected older religious and spiritual traditions and situated their development activities beside traditional sacred places, due to their power and potency. MQI's Itikaf took place beside the Sufi Syed Tahir Alauddin Al-Qadri Shrine and Kalani's vision was inspired by the sacred Hawaiian heiau and halau sites on the property. Many of the organisations we studied also had digital 'third spaces' (Hoover and Echchaibi 2012), which complemented and provided information about their real world activities that in some cases questioned and usurped dominant capitalist and/or patriarchal narratives. In MQI's case, they also sought to address misinformation and negative stereotypes about Islam.

Participants considered both built and natural spaces to be sacred and while the Kalani case study can be most obviously linked with theories of therapeutic landscapes, the gardens at SDKM also have similar qualities of being calming spaces. The Medicine Buddha Temple at SDKM and the Syed Tahir Alauddin Al-Qadri and Data Darbar Shrine sites were also described as sites of healing and reflection.

We certainly also observed a 'co-production of religion and place across a range of contexts, scales, and networks' (Hopkins et al. 2013) in which religious and spiritual teachings inspired the use of sacred places as development spaces in all of our case studies. The participants' stories of the places in which they conducted their activities, provided us with deep insights regarding their significance. These personal accounts often included references to teachings of the founders of their tradition, their own teachers who established the sacred places in which they now live and/or work, and also the original founders of the religions that they now practice. These stories provide guidance of how and where to live ethically and particularly of how and where to help those in need and of sustainable stewardship of land.

Sacred places and development spaces

The case studies within this book have covered a range of geographic regions, religious and spiritual communities, as well as socio-economic development activities. But across this variety of locations, religions, and community development activities it was clear there were some common attributes that enhanced the likelihood of these sacred places to be appropriate and successful development spaces.

Locality

As stated above, sacred places are commonplace the world over. Grand religious buildings hundreds of years old can be found in cities and rural locations alike. Even more common are local sacred places, built by and for local communities for their own worship needs. These places are generally situated in local towns and villages and are *a part* of those communities more so than being *apart* from them. Community members recognise these places as part of their community infrastructure and as resources to support the community. Typically, these religious buildings and places are located centrally to the town or village and are easily accessible by community members. It is for these reasons of *locality* that sacred places make good development spaces. Even if these places are of a different religion – see the Australian chapter for example – to the participants and recipients of the development activity, the buildings and places are familiar due to their location. Despite the unexpected outcomes of providing HIV and AIDS care and prevention training some distance away from the community described in the Preface of this volume, ease of access is an important factor in delivery of successful community development outcomes. Whether that access be by private or public transport, being able to access these places is a pre-requisite for participation.

Security

Community members participating in community development activities located within sacred places stated across the range of case studies that these religious buildings and places provide a sense of security and sanctuary. Again, by the very nature of their original purpose, such feelings that are engendered are not unexpected. Despite the negative impact religious beliefs and practices can have (as discussed in the Introduction of this volume) they can also provide a sense of security and safety to adherents. Traditionally, many religious buildings have been sites of sanctuary where people have sought protection from external threats. As the case studies illustrate, such sanctuary and security can still be found. In the case study of Vanuatu, this sanctuary is very much a physical protection (from cyclones), whilst in the Stand Up case study the participants felt that the church was a safe place for their activities. By feeling safe and secure, community members are more likely to fully engage in the activity and be willing to take risks or extend their own practices around health, education, sanitation, etc. as part of a community development programme. Security and safety can also result in wider participation of the community.

Belonging

Religious identification is clearly something that is important with such an overwhelming proportion of the global population self-identifying as having religious affiliation and belief. Levels of religious adherence and participation in formalised religious worship activities will vary from adherent to adherent, the case studies contained in this volume do illustrate that there is a reported sense of 'belonging' when meeting in a religious place. There is familiarity with the architecture and furnishings and expected norms around dress and behaviour. As a community hub, many community members congregate around these sacred places for more than simply the purpose of worship, further strengthening a spirit of belonging. Indeed, as reported in the Australian case study, even if the sacred place is not of the same religion as the community members (or community facilitators), there remains a cultural familiarity with these buildings and places built up over a lifetime of attending a range of community and family events, such as weddings, funerals, and so forth. Thus, on this occasion, Muslim women felt comfortable and at home within the Christian church and their familiarity with the physical space translated to a sense of belonging and ease with the community development activities being undertaken. Their sense of belonging was also aided by active interfaith networks that made all people of faith and no-faith feel welcome in the city of Dandenong.

Narrative

When undertaking development activities in partnership with communities in which faith plays a significant role, it is important to develop an understanding not only of the communities' religious beliefs and rituals but also the places that are sacred to these communities. This can only be learned by listening to people's stories, and to narratives which they hold sacred. In each of the case studies presented in this volume, participants explained how and why places were significant, how and why they were constructed, and why development activities were conducted within and beside them with reference to teachings and practices that had preceded them. The sacredness of places is often multilayered, hybrid and complex. Before undertaking a new wave of development activity, our research indicates that it would be wise to become familiar with existing and past traditions and to treat them, and the sacred places that are important to them, respectfully. Taking the time to do so is likely to maximise the success of future development activities.

Engagement

Closely linked with the sense of belonging to activities and events that occur in religious places, is a natural feeling of close engagement with those activities. The simple act of housing these activities within sacred places has enhanced people's engagement and sense of purpose. There is an extension of people's own personal relationship with these places of worship to that of activities that sit outside traditional worship activities, but remain located within the same sacred place. Whilst these community development activities are distinct from acts of worship normally associated with sacred places, commitment to the success of these activities is heightened within community members precisely because they are occurring within these buildings and places. If there is an alignment between the religious tenets and teachings and the activities being undertaken then this engagement and commitment is further enhanced (see Clarke et al. 2011).

Appropriateness

There is a long history of religious organisations, bodies or individuals imbued with religious fervour assisting more vulnerable members of their communities. Indeed, many non-governmental organisations formally working within the development sector have religious roots (Rae and Clarke 2013). It is not unsurprising to active members of religious congregations that there are many community development activities being supported by, or run by, or occurring in religious communities. This volume has provided a number of examples of activities that are clearly focused on temporal wellbeing as well as, and sometimes ahead of, spiritual wellbeing that are occurring within religious places. However, because of this long history, across all the world's major religions, of addressing the material wellbeing of the most vulnerable, there is not just a level of acceptance but almost an expectation that such activities occur under the guise of religion. These activities are seen as appropriate and proper and thus have wide social support. The Vanuatu case study describes the institutionalisation of such work through the establishment of the Presbyterian Women's

Missionary Union, as does the large scale of the MQI development activities taking place beside the shrines in Lahore.

Across the globe, people hold religious beliefs. As a result of these beliefs, physical structures are built, virtual forums are developed and natural environments are identified in which religious worship takes place. These sacred places are many and generally found in close proximity to those who utilise them. In both wealthy and poor countries, sacred places are being used as spaces for community and personal development activities to occur. This volume has presented a wide range of case studies from across the Asia-Pacific region that illustrate how these sacred places positively impact upon the delivery of these activities. In the absence of a strong theory of place and space within the field of development studies, these case studies point to the effectiveness of sacred places as development spaces because of locality, security, belonging, narrative, engagement and appropriateness. This series of case studies also provides further empirical evidence of the positive role that religion can play in the development sector and support for a greater visibility of religion within this endeavour – a visibility that is slowly occurring but has been too long in coming.

Our research has demonstrated that development is a process, which occurs within and across places, through partnerships of diverse actors who share a commitment to social justice and sustainable development. These partnerships create development spaces that recognise not only the intersectional nature of social and environmental issues but also the need for multidimensional strategies to address them effectively. These strategies have been situated in diverse real world and digital places that have influenced their development, and they are increasingly vital now to mitigate pressing risks of poverty, climate change, gender inequity and violent extremism that continue to threaten our societies.

The modern study of development has evolved since its first incarnation halfway through the last century. There is now much stronger understanding – based on rigorous empirical evidence – of the process of economic and social development, which has led to a professionalisation of those working at the local and international levels to improve the lives of the poor. Over this time, there have been improvements as well in how issues of gender, the environment, sustainability, diversity, maternal and child health, disaster preparedness, HIV and AIDS, child work and child labour, sanitation, and microfinance are all addressed and more optimally operationalised in development programming, led by or at least in partnership with, local communities. So whilst the 'how' and 'why' questions of development have been considered, what has lagged though is focused attention on 'where' development takes place. As this volume hopefully demonstrates, the place of development is paramount to its success.

References

Chidester, D. & Linenthal, E.T. 1995, 'Introduction', in D. Chidester & E.T. Linenthal (eds.), *American sacred space*, Indiana University Press, Bloomington, pp. 1–42.

Clarke, M. 2011, *Development and religion: Theology and practice*, Edward Elgar, Cheltenham.

Clarke, M., Charnley, S. & Lumbers, J. 2011, 'Churches, mosques and condoms: Understanding successful faith-based organisations' HIV and AIDS interventions', *Development in Practice*, vol. 21, no. 1, pp. 3–17.

Grusin, R. (ed.) 2015, *The nonhuman* turn, University of Minnesota Press, Minneapolis.

Hoover, S.M. & Echchaibi, N. 2012, *The 'third space' of digital religion*, viewed 4 July 2014, http://cmrc.colorado.edu/wp-content/uploads/2012/03/Third-Spaces-Essay-Draft-Final.pdf.

Hopkins, P., Kong, L. & Olson, E. 2013, *Religion and space: Landscape, politics and peity*, Springer, Dordrecht.

Kong, L. 1990, 'Geography and religion: Trends and prospects', *Progress in Human Geography*, vol. 14, no. 3, pp. 355–371.

Kong, L. 2001, 'Mapping "new" geographies of religion: Politics and poetics in modernity', *Progress in Human Geography*, vol. 25, no. 2, pp. 211–233.

Kong, L. 2010, 'Global shifts, theoretical shifts: Changing geographies of religion', *Progress in Human Geography*, vol. 34, no. 6, pp. 755–776.

Lane, B.C. 2002, *Landscapes of the sacred: Geography and narrative in American spirituality (expanded edition)*, The John Hopkins University Press, Baltimore and London.

Pew Research Centre 2012, *Global religious landscape*, viewed 20 November 2015, http://www.pewforum.org/files/2014/01/global-religion-full.pdf.

Rabinow, P. 1984, *The Foucault reader*, Pantheon, New York.

Rae, L. & Clarke, M. 2013, 'Australian development FBOs and NGOs', in M. Clarke (ed.), *Handbook of research on religion and development*, Edward Elgar, London, pp. 570–584.

Soja, E.W. 1989, *Postmodern geographies: The reassertion of space in critical social theory*, Verso, London.

Bibliography

Alliance for Bhikkunis n.d., Home, viewed on 7 July 2015, http://www.bhikkhuni.net.

Alkire, S. & Foster, J. 2011, 'Counting and multidimensional poverty measurement', *Journal of Public Economics*, vol. 95, no. 7–8, pp. 476–487.

Alolo, N. & Connell, J. 2013, 'Indigenous religions and development: African traditional religions', in M. Clarke (ed.), *Handbook of research on religion and development*, Edward Elgar, Cheltenham, pp. 138–163.

Ammerman, N. 1996, 'Organized religion in a voluntaristic society', *Sociology of Religion*, vol. 58, no. 3, pp. 203–215.

Ammerman, N. 2003, 'Religious identities and institutions', in M. Dillon (ed.), *Handbook of the sociology of religion*, Cambridge University Press, Cambridge, pp. 207–224.

Ammerman, N. 2007, *Everyday religion: Observing modern religious lives*, Oxford University Press, Oxford.

Ammerman, N. 2013a, *Sacred stories, spiritual tribes: Finding religion in everyday life*, Oxford University Press, New York.

Ammerman, N. 2013b, 'Spiritual but not religious? Beyond binary choices in the study of religion', *Journal for the Scientific Study of Religion*, vol. 52, no. 2, pp. 258–278.

Anttonen, V. 2003, 'Sacred sites as markers of difference – Exploring cognitive foundations of territoriality', in L. Tarkka (ed.), *Dynamics of tradition: Perspectives on oral poetry and folk belief*, The Finnish Literature Society, Helsinki, pp. 291–305.

Appleby, S.R. 2000, *The ambivalence of the sacred: Religion, violence, and reconciliation*, Rowman and Littlefield, Lanham.

Appleby, S.R. 2003, 'Retrieving the missing dimension of statecraft: Religious faith in the service of peacebuilding', in D. Johnston (ed.), *Faith-based diplomacy: Trumping realpolitik*, Oxford University Press, Oxford, pp. 231–258.

Beaglehole, J.C. 1966, *The exploration of the Pacific*, Stanford University Press, London.

Bader, V. 2007, *Secularism or democracy? Associational governance of religious diversity*, Amsterdam University Press, Amsterdam.

Bainbridge, W.S. 1997, *The sociology of religious movements*, Routledge, New York.

Beck, U. 2006, *The cosmopolitan vision*, Polity Press, Cambridge.

Beckford, J.A. 1990, 'The sociology of religion and social problems', *Sociological Analysis*, vol. 51, no. 1, pp. 1–14.

Beckford, J.A. 2003, *Social theory and religion*, Cambridge University Press, Cambridge.

Bhabha, H.K. 1994, *The location of culture*, Routledge, London.

Bhabja, H.K. 1990, 'The third space: Interview with Homi Bhabha', in J. Rutherford (ed.), *Identity: Community, culture, difference*, Lawrence and Wishart, London, pp. 207–221.

Boff, L. 1987, *Introducing liberation theology*, Orbis Books, Maryknoll.

Bouma, G.D. 1995, 'The emergence of religious plurality in Australia: A multicultural society', *Sociology of Religion*, vol. 56, no. 4, pp. 285–302.

Bouma, G.D. (ed.) 1997, *Many religions, all Australian: Religious settlement, identity and cultural diversity*, The Christian Research Association, Melbourne.

Bouma, G.D. 2006, *Australian soul: Religion and spirituality in the 21st century*, Cambridge University Press, Cambridge.

Bourdieu, P. 1977, *Outline of a theory of practice*, trans. R. Nice, Cambridge University Press, Cambridge, original work published 1972.

Büttner, M. 1980, 'On the history and philosophy of the geography of religion in Germany', *Religion*, vol. 10, no. 1, pp. 86–119.

Campbell, H. 2005, *Exploring religious community online: We are one in the network*, Peter Lang, New York.

Campbell, H. (ed.) 2013, *Digital religion: Understanding religious practice in new media worlds*, Routledge, London and New York.

Campbell, R.A. 2006, 'Theodicy, distribution of risk, and reflexive modernisation: Explaining the cultural significance of new religious movements', in J.A. Beckford & J. Walliss (eds.), *Theorising religion: Classical and contemporary debates*, Ashgate, Aldershot, pp. 90–104.

Campbell, N. & Oldmeadow, M. (2006), *Tall tress to Trinity*, mimeo. Trinity Uniting Church, Dandenong.

Casanova, J. 1994, *Public religions in the modern world*, University of Chicago Press, Chicago.

Casanova, J. 2001, 'Religion, the new millennium, and globalization', *Sociology of Religion*, vol. 62, no. 4, pp. 415–441.

Chambers, R. 1983, *Rural development: Putting the last first*, Longman, Harlow.

Chambers, R. 2005, *Ideas for development*, Earthscan, London.

Chidester, D. & Linenthal, E.T. 1995, 'Introduction', in D. Chidester & E.T. Linenthal (eds.), *American sacred space*, Indiana University Press, Bloomington, pp. 1–42.

City of Greater Dandenong (CDG) 2015, *Statistical data for Victorian communities, Summary of social conditions in greater Dandenong*, viewed 20 October 2015, http://www.greaterdandenong.com/document/18464/statistical-data-for-victorian-communities.

Clarke, M. 2011, *Development and religion: Theology and practice*, Edward Elgar, Cheltenham.

Clarke, M. (ed.) 2012, *Mission and development: God's work or good works?* Continuum Books, London.

Clarke, M. 2013, 'Good works and God's work: A case study of churches and community development in Vanuatu', *Asia Pacific Viewpoint*, vol. 54, no. 3, pp. 340–351.

Clarke, M. (ed.) 2013, *Handbook of research on development and religion*, Edward Elgar, Cheltenham.

Clarke, M. 2015, 'Christianity and the shaping of Vanuatu's social and political development', *Journal of the Academic Study of Religion*, vol. 28, no. 1, pp. 24–41.

Clarke, M., Charnley, S. & Lumbers, J. 2011, 'Churches, mosques and condoms: Understanding successful faith-based organisations' HIV and AIDS interventions,' *Development in Practice*, vol. 21, no. 1, pp. 3–17.

Clarke, M., Feeny, S., & Donnelly, J. 2014, 'Water, sanitation and hygiene interventions in the Pacific: Defining, assessing and improving "Sustainability"', *European Journal of Development Research*, vol. 26, no. 5, pp. 692–706.

Clarke, M. & Ware, V. 2015, 'Understanding faith-based organisations: How FBOs are contrasted with NGOs in international development literature', *Progress in Development Studies*, vol. 15, no. 1, pp. 37–48.

Conradson 2007, 'The experiential economy of stillness: Places of retreat in contemporary Britain', in A.M. Williams (ed), *Therapeutic landscapes*, Ashgate, Aldershot, pp. 33–48.

Craig, D. & Porter, D. 1997, 'Framing participation: Development projects, professionals, and organizations', *Development in Practice*, vol. 7, no. 3, pp. 229–236.

Daily Post (2015), 'Include Churches in Gov't recovery management framework: VCC', *Daily Post*, 3 June, p. 5.

Deneulin, S. & Bano, M. 2009, *Religion in development: Rewriting the secular script*, Zed Books, London.

Dhammananda, B.Kabilsingh, C.) 2007, *Beyond gender*, Foundation for Women, Law and Rural Development and Women's Studies Centre, Faculty of Social Sciences, Chiang Mai University, Chiang Mai.

Dhammananda, B.Kabilsingh, C.) 2012, *Herstory*, Thai Tibet Centre, Bangkok.

Dhammananda, B.Kabilsingh, C.) 2014, 'Bhikkhuni Ta Tao: Paving the way for future generations', in K.L. Tsomo (ed.) *Eminent Buddhist women*, State University of New York Press, New York, pp. 61–70.

Eliade, M. 1961, *Sacred and profane*, trans. W.R. Tiask, Harcourt, Brace, New York, original work published 1957.

Eriksen, A. 2015, *Gender, Christianity and change in Vanuatu: An analysis of social movements in North Ambrym*, Ashgate, Aldershot.

Fang, X. & Bi, L. 2013, 'Confucianism', in M. Clarke (ed.), *Handbook of research on religion and development*, Edward Elgar, Cheltenham, pp. 124–137.

Fenn, M.L. & Koppedrayer, K. 2008, 'Sakyadhita: A transnational gathering place for Buddhist women', *Journal of Global Buddhism*, vol. 9, pp. 45–48.

Feeny, S. (ed.) 2014, *Household vulnerability and resilience to economic shocks: Findings from Melanesia*, Ashgate, Farnham.

Food and Agricultural Organization (FAO) 2014, The state of food insecurity in the world 2014: Strengthening the enabling Environment for food security and nutrition, viewed 20 November 2015, http://www.fao.org/publications/sofi/2014/en.

Forum on Religion and Ecology (FORE) n.d., Forum on religion and ecology at Yale University, viewed 20 December 2015, http://fore.yale.edu.

Fountain, P., Bush, R. & Feener, R. (eds.) 2015, *Religion and the politics of development*, Palgrave Macmillan, Basingstoke.

Fox, J. & Sandler, S. (eds.) 2006, *Religion in world conflict*, Routledge, London.

Gesler, W. 2005, 'Editorial, therapeutic lansdscapes: An emmerging theme', *Health & Place*, vol. 11, no. 4, pp. 295–297.

Glacken, C.J. 1956, 'Changing ideas of the habitable world', in W.L. Thomas, Jr, (ed.), *Man's role in changing the face of the earth*, University of Chicago Press, Chicago, pp. 70–92.

Glacken, C.J. 1967, *Traces on the Rhodian shore*, University of California Press, Berkeley.

Gosha-e-Durood (GeD) n.d.a, *About-Gosha-e-Durood*, viewed 10 February 2015, http://www.gosha-e-durood.com/english/tid/16131/About-Gosha-e-Durood.html.

Gosha-e-Durood (GeD) n.d.b, *Minara-tus-Salam (Gosha-e-Durood) building*, viewed 10 February 2015, http://www.gosha-e-durood.com/english/tid/23050.

Goulet, D. 1980, 'Development experts: The one-eyed giants', *World Development*, vol. 8, nos. 6–7, pp. 481–489.

Gross, R.M. 1993, *Buddhism after patriarchy: A feminist history, analysis, and reconstruction of Buddhism*, State University of New York Press, Albany.

Grusin, R. (ed.) 2015, *The nonhuman turn*, University of Minnesota Press, Minneapolis.

Gunder Frank, A. 1967, *Capitalism and underdevelopment in Latin America*, Monthly Review Press, New York.

Gutierrez, G. 1973, *A theology of liberation*, Orbis Books, Maryknoll.

Habermas, J. 1981, 'New social movements', *Telos*, vol. 49, pp. 33–37.

Habermas, J. 1998, 'Learning by disaster? A diagnostic look back on the short 20th century', *Constellations*, vol. 5, no. 3, pp. 307–320.

Habermas, J. 2006, 'Religion in the public sphere', *European Journal of Philosophy*, vol. 14, no. 1, pp. 1–25.

Habermas, J. 2008, 'Notes on a post-secular society', sightandsound.com, 18 June 2008, viewed 10 February 2015, http://www.signandsight.com/features/1714.html.

Halafoff, A. 2013, *The multifaith movement: Global risks and cosmopolitan solutions.* Springer, Dordrecht.

Harvey, D. 1989, *The condition of postmodernity: An enquiry into the origins of cultural change*, Blackwell, Oxford.

Harvey, D. 2004, 'Space as a key word', paper for Marx and Philosophy Conference, 29 May 2004, Institute of Education, London.

Haynes, J. 2007, *An introduction to international relations and religion*, Pearson and Longman, Harlow.

Hedges, P. & Halafoff, A. 2015, 'Globalisation and multifaith societies', *Studies in Interreligious Dialogue*, vol. 25, no. 2, pp. 135-161

Hervieu-Léger, D. 2000, *Religion as a chain of memory*, Polity, Cambridge.

Hilliard, D. 1978, *Gods gentlemen: A history of the Melanesian Mission 1849–1942*, University of Queensland Press, Brisbane.

Hoover, S.M. & Echchaibi, N. 2012, *The 'third space' of digital religion*, viewed 4 July 2014, http://cmrc.colorado.edu/wp-content/uploads/2012/03/Third-Spaces-Essay-Draft-Final.pdf.

Hopkins, P., Kong, L. & Olson, E. 2013, *Religion and space: Landscape, politics and peity*, Springer, Dordrecht.

Hoyez, A. 2007, 'From Rishikesh to Yogaville: The globalization of therapeutic landscapes', in A.M. Williams (ed.), *Therapeutic landscapes*, Ashgate, Aldershot. pp. 49–64.

Ife, J. 2013, *Community development in an uncertain world*, Cambridge University Press, Cambridge.

Isaac, E. 1959–60, 'Religion, landscape and space,' *Landscape*, vol. 9, no. 4, pp. 14–18.

Isaac, E. 1965, *Religious geography and the geography of religion*, in Man and the Earth, University of Colorado Studies, Series in Earth Sciences No. 3, University of Colorado Press, Boulder.

Itikaf City n.d.a, *About*, viewed 10 February 2015, http://www.itikaf.com/english/tid/14303/itikaf-city-by-minhaj-ul-quran-international.html.

Itikaf City n.d.b, *Contact us*, viewed 10 February 2015, http://www.itikaf.com/english/tid/14324/contact-details-itikaf-city-of-minhaj-ul-quran.html.

Jackson, R. 2014, *'Signposts': Policy and practice for teaching about religions and non-religious worldviews in intercultural education*, Council of Europe, Strasbourg.

Jennings, M. 2014 'Bridging the local and the global: Faith-based organisations as non-state providers in Tanzania', in M. Cammett & L.M. MacLean (eds.), *The politics of non-state social welfare*, Cornell University Press, Ithaca, pp. 119–136.

Jewish Aid Australia (JAA) 2012, *Annual Report 2012: Connecting the Dots*, viewed 8 October 2015, https://jewishaidaustralia.files.wordpress.com/2012/11/jaa-annual-report-2012.pdf.

Juergensmeyer, M. 2008, *Global rebellion: Religious challenges to the secular state, from Christian militias to Al Qaeda*, University of California Press, Berkeley.

Juergensmeyer, M. 2010, 'The global rise of religious nationalism', *Australian Journal of International Affairs*, vol. 64, no. 3, pp. 262–273.

Kabilsingh, C. 1998, *Buddhism and nature conservation*, Thai Tibet Centre, Phra Nakorn.

Kalani n.d. *Home*, viewed 1 February 2015 https://kalani.com.

Kaldor, M. 1999, *New & old wars: Organized violence in a global era*, Polity, Cambridge.

Kaldor, M. 2003, *Global civil society: An answer to war*, Polity, Cambridge.

Kearns, L. & Keller, C. (eds.) 2007, *Ecospirit: Religions and philosophies for the earth*, Fordham University Press, New York.

Kettell, S. 2013, 'Faithless: The politics of New Atheism', *Secularism and Nonreligion*, vol. 2, pp. 61–72.

Kingsbury, D., McKay, J., Hunt, J., McGillivray, M. & Clarke, M. 2011, *International development*, Palgrave-MacMillian, London.

Knott, K. 2005, *The location of religion: A spatial analysis*, Equinox, London.

Koob, R. 2014, *Kalani: A leap of faith, hope and love*, Kalani Publishers, Pahoa.

Kong, L. 1990, 'Geography and religion: Trends and prospects', *Progress in Human Geography*, vol. 14, no. 3, pp. 355–371.

Kong, L. 2001, 'Mapping "new" geographies of religion: Politics and poetics in modernity', *Progress in Human Geography*, vol. 25, no. 2, pp. 211–233.

Kong, L. 2010, 'Global shifts, theoretical shifts: Changing geographies of religion', *Progress in Human Geography*, vol. 34, no. 6, pp. 755–776.

Kustiani 2013, 'Examining the date of Mahāpajāpatī's Ordination', in K.L. Tsomo (ed.), *Buddhism at the grassroots, 13th Sakyadhita international conference on Buddhist women*, Sakyadhita International Association of Buddhist Women, New Delhi, pp. 124–127.

Lane, B.C. 2002, *Landscapes of the sacred: Geography and narrative in American spirituality (expanded edition)*, The John Hopkins University Press, Baltimore and London.

Leach, M., Scambary, J., Clarke, M., Feeny, S. & Wallace, H. 2013, *Attitudes to national identity in Melanesia and Timor-Leste: A survey of future leaders in Papua New Guinea, Solomon Islands, Vanuatu, and Timor-Leste*, Peter Lang, Oxford.

Leaman, O. 2006, *Jewish thought*, Routledge, New York.

Levi-Strauss, C. 1950, 'Introduction à l'œuvre de Marcel Mauss', in M. Mauss, *Sociologie et anthropologie*, Presses universitaires de France, Paris, pp. IX–LII.

Marshall, K. & Keough, L. 2004, *Mind, heart, and soul in the fight against poverty*, The World Bank, Washington.

Marty, M.E. & Appleby, R.S. 1992, *The glory and the power: The fundamentalist challenge to the modern world*, Beacon Press, Boston.

Massam, K. 2014, 'Creating spaces between: Women and mission in Oceania', Keynote Address, Conference of the Association for Practical Theology in Oceania, Sydney, 27–30 November 2014.

Mazumdar, S. & Mazumdar, S. 2012, 'Immigrant home gardens: Places of religion, culture, ecology, and family', *Landscape and Urban Planning*, vol. 105, no. 3, pp. 258–265.

Mazumdar, S. & Mazumdar, S. 2009, 'Religion, immigration, and home making in diaspora: Hindu space in Southern California', *Journal of Environmental Psychology*, vol. 29, no. 2, pp. 256–266.

McGillivray, M. 2012, 'What is development', in D. Kingsbury, J. McKay, J. Hunt, M. McGillivray & M. Clarke, *International development, issues and challenges*, Palgrave, London, pp. 23–52.

McGregor, A., Skeaff, A., & Bevan, M. 2012, 'Overcoming secularism? Catholic development geographies in Timor-Leste,' *Third World Quarterly*, vol. 33, no. 6, pp. 1129–1146.

McGuire, M. 1997, *Religion: The social context*, Belmont, Wadsworth.

McGuire, M. 2008, *Lived religion, faith and practice in everyday life*, Oxford University Press, Oxford.

Miles, W.F.S. 1998, *Bridging mental boundaries in a post-colonial microcosm: Identity and development in Vanuatu*, University of Hawaii Press, Honolulu.

Miller, J. 2013, 'Daoism and development', in M. Clarke (ed.), *Handbook of research on religion and development*, Edward Elgar, Cheltenham, pp. 113–123.

Minhaj-ul-Quran International (MQI) n.d.a, *A profile of Shaykh-ul-Islam Dr Muhammad Tahir-ul-Qadri*, viewed 10 February 2015, http://www.minhaj.org/english/tid/8718/A-Profile-of-Shaykh-ul-Islam-Dr-Muhammad-Tahir-ul-Qadri.html.

Minhaj-ul-Quran International (MQI) n.d.b, *About, Introduction, Minhaj-ul-Quran-International*, viewed 10 February 2015, http://www.minhaj.org/english/tid/1799/Minhaj-ul-Quran-International.html.

Minhaj Welfare Foundation (MWF) n.d.a, *About*, viewed 10 February 2015, http://www.welfare.org.pk/english/tid/8723/About-MWF.html.

Minhaj Welfare Foundation (MWF) n.d.b, *Aghosh orphan care*, viewed 10 February 2015, http://www.welfare.org.pk/english/tid/3533/Aghosh-%28Orphan-Care-Home%29.html.

Minhaj Welfare Foundation (MWF) n.d.c, *Ongoing projects*, viewed 10 February 2015, http://www.welfare.org.pk/english/tid/24681/Ongoing-Projects.html.

Minhaj Welfare Foundation (MWF) n.d.d, *Qurbani program*, viewed 10 February 2015, http://www.welfare.org.pk/english/tid/34221/Minhaj-Welfare-Foundation-Qurbani-Program-2015-meat-distribution-poor-people-refugees.html.

Orsi, R.A. 2005, *Between heaven and earth: The religious world's people make and the scholars who study hem*, Princeton University Press, Princeton.

Otto, R. 1950, *The idea of the holy*, trans. J.W. Harley, Oxford University Press, London.

Pew Research Centre 2012, *Global religious landscape*, viewed 20 November 2015, http://www.pewforum.org/files/2014/01/global-religion-full.pdf.

Presbyterian Missionary Women's Union (PWMU) 2014, *PWMU Five Year Plan, 2014–2018*, PWMU, Port Vila.

Rabinow, P. 1984, *The Foucault reader*, Pantheon, New York.

Rist, G. 2014, *The history of development*, Zed Books, London.

Rae, L. & Clarke, M. 2013, 'Australian development FBOs and NGOs', in M. Clarke, (ed.), *Handbook of research on religion and development*, Edward Elgar, London. 570–584

Rees, J. 2011, *Religion in international politics and development: The World Bank and faith institutions*, Edward Elgar, Cheltenham.

Regenvanu, S. 2004, *Laef blong mi: From village to nation*, University of South Pacific Press, Suva.

Roser, M. (2015) 'World Poverty', *OurWorldInData.org*, viewed 20 November 2015, http://ourworldindata.org/data/growth-and-distribution-of-prosperity/world-poverty.

Rostow, W. 1960, *The stages of economic growth*, Cambridge University Press, Cambridge.
Sakyadhita n.d., *Home*, viewed on 7 July 2015, http://www.sakyadhita.org.
Segal, E. 2009, *Introducing Judaism*, Routledge, London.
Seiple, R. & Hoover, D. (eds.) 2004, *Religion and security: The new nexus in international relations*, Rowman and Littlefield, Lanham.
Sen, A. 1999, *Development as freedom*, Oxford University Press, New York.
Shaykh-ul-IslamDr Muhammad Tahir-ul-Qadri 2011, *Profile of Shaykh-ul-Islam*, viewed 10 February 2015, http://www.drtahirulqadri.com/main/profile-of-shaykh-ul-islam.
Sihlongonyane, M.F. 2003, 'The rhetoric of the community in project management: The case of Mohlakeng township', *Development in Practice*, vol. 11, no. 1, pp. 34–44.
Soja, Ew 1989, *Postmodern geographies: The reassertion of space in critical social theory*, Verso, London.
Soja, Ew 1996, *Thirdspace: Journeys to Los Angeles and other real and imagined places*, Blackwell, Oxford.
Songdhammakalyani Monastery n.d. *Home*, viewed on 7 July 2015, http://www.thaibhikkhunis.org/eng2014/contact.html.
Stiglitz, J.E. 1999, 'The role of participation in development', *Development Outreach*, Summer 1999 1999, World Bank, Washington, pp. 1–4.
Taylor, C. 2009, 'Foreword: What is secularism?' in G.B. Levey & T. Modood (eds.), *Secularism, religion and multicultural citizenship*, Cambridge University Press, Cambridge, pp. xi–xxii.
ter Haar, G. (ed.) 2011, *Religion and development: Ways of transforming the world*, Hurst Publications, London.
Tomalin, E., Starkey, C. & Halafoff, A. 2015 'Cyber sisters: Buddhist women's online activism and practice', in D. Enstedt, G. Larrson & E. Pace (eds.), *Religion and internet*, Annual Review of the Sociology of Religion Series vol. 6, Brill, Leiden and Boston, pp. 11–33.
Truman, H. 1949, Inaugural address, viewed 8 October 2015, https://www.trumanlibrary.org/whistlestop/50yr_archive/inagural20jan1949.htm.
Tsomo, K.L. 2009, *Buddhist women in a global multicultural community*, Sukhi Hotu Press, Kuala Lumpur.
United Nations n. d., *Millenium development goals*, viewed 20 December 2015, http://www.un.org/millenniumgoals.
United Nations 2015, *Sustainable development goals*, viewed 20 December 2015, http://www.un.org/sustainabledevelopment/sustainable-development-goals.
United Nations Children's Fund (UNICEF) 2015, 'Cyclone Pam in Vanuatu', viewed 21 July 2015, www.unicef.org.nz/vanuatu.
United Nations Developemnt Programme (UNDP) 1990, *Human development report*, UNDP, New York.
United Nations News 2015, 'Cyclone Pam: UN agency reports all 22 Vanuatu islands reached with relief supplies', viewed 21 July 2015, http://www.un.org/apps/news/story.asp?NewsID=50440#.Va2SquvIvuV.
Urry, J. 1985, 'Social relations, space and time,' in D. Gregory and J. Urry (eds.), *Social relations and spatial structures*, St. Martin's Press, New York, pp. 21–48.
van der Leeuw, G. (1938) *Religion in essence and manifestation*, trans. J.E. lbrner, Princeton University Press, Princeton, original work published in German 1933.
Vanuatu Christian Council (VCC) and Act for Peace 2015, 'Vanuatu Christian evacuation centres need support', viewed 23 July 2015, https://www.youtube.com/watch?v=8plVMQa0uEU.

Vanuatu National Statistical Office (NSO) 2009, *2009 National census of population and housing*, viewed 1 July 2012, http://www.vnso.gov.vu/images/stories/2009_Census_Summary_release_final.pdf.

Watson, B. & Clarke, M. 2014, *Child sponsorship: Exploring pathways to a brighter future*, Palgrave MacMillan, London.

Willaime, J.P. 2006, 'Religion in ultramodernity', in J.A. Beckford & J. Walliss (eds.), *Theorising religion: Classical and contemporary debates*, Ashgate, Aldershot, pp. 77–89.

Williams, A.M. 2007, 'Introduction: The continuing maturation of the therapeutic landscape concept', in A.M. Williams (ed.), *Therapeutic Landscapes*, Ashgate, Aldershot. 1-12

World Bank 2015, *Global monitoring report 2015/2016: Development goals in an era of demographic change*, viewed 20 November 2015, http://pubdocs.worldbank.org/pubdocs/publicdoc/2015/10/503001444058224597/Global-Monitoring-Report-2015.pdf.

Woodhead, L. 2011, 'Five concepts of religion', *International Review of Sociology: Revue Internationale de Sociologie*, vol. 21, no. 1, pp. 121–143.

Woodward, K. 2014, *A political memoir of the Anglo-French condominium of the New Hebrides*, ANU Press, Canberra.

Yogini Project n.d. Home, viewed on 7 July 2015, http://theyoginiproject.org.

Index

For Product Safety Concerns and Information please contact our EU
representative GPSR@taylorandfrancis.com
Taylor & Francis Verlag GmbH, Kaufingerstraße 24, 80331 München, Germany

www.ingramcontent.com/pod-product-compliance
Ingram Content Group UK Ltd.
Pitfield, Milton Keynes, MK11 3LW, UK
UKHW020947180425
457613UK00019B/559